William V. Wallace

Maritana

William V. Wallace

Maritana

ISBN/EAN: 9783337042325

Printed in Europe, USA, Canada, Australia, Japan

Cover: Foto ©Thomas Meinert / pixelio.de

More available books at **www.hansebooks.com**

MARITANA.

Opera in Three Acts.

WRITTEN BY

EDWARD FITZBALL.

MUSIC COMPOSED

BY

W. VINCENT WALLACE.

THE FULL LIBRETTO ADAPTED, WITH BUSINESS AND STAGE DIRECTIONS, BY

LEON KEACH.

BOSTON:

OLIVER DITSON COMPANY.

NEW YORK:	CHICAGO:	PHILADELPHIA:	BOSTON:
C. H. DITSON & CO.	LYON & HEALY.	J. E. DITSON & CO.	JOHN C. HAYNES & CO.

DRAMATIS PERSONÆ.

CHARLES II., (King of Spain) .... BASS.	ALCADE, ... BASS.
DON JOSE DE SANTAREM, (His Minister) BARITONE.	CAPTAIN OF GUARDS, ... BASS
DON CÆSAR DE BAZAN, ... TENOR.	MARITANA, (A Gitana) .... SOPRANO.
MARQUIS DE MONTEFIORI, ... BASS.	MARCHIONESS DE MONTEFIORI, ... SOPRANO.
LAZARILLO, ... MEZZO SOPRANO.	

Nobles, Alguazils, Soldiers, Men-at-Arms, Populace, Gipsies.

SCENE.—Madrid. .... Time of Representation,—*Three Hours.*

ARGUMENT.

In a public square of the city of Madrid, a band of gipsies are levying contributions on the populace, in recompense for the songs and dances with which they amuse them. With this tribe is MARITANA, a young girl of extraordinary beauty of person, and a vocalist of more than common talent. The gay King, CHARLES THE SECOND of Spain, has seen her, and is smitten with her charms. At the end of one of her lays, he gives her a coin of value, and hastens away; but his disguise does not conceal him from the keen eyes of DON JOSE, his minister, who, to carry oöt his own designs upon the Queen, resolves to aid in converting the fair young gipsy to the purposes of the King. He praises her beauty, excites her ambition, and awakens in her heart hopes of future grandeur and prosperity. At this moment, DON CÆSAR DE BAZAN comes reeling from a tavern, where he has lost his last maravedi in gambling. His costume, once rich, is now ragged and dirty; his handsome person bears marks of dissipation and poverty; yet, in his air and bearing, there is still something noble and prepossessing. Don Jose and he have been friends in brighter days, and recognizing each other, Don Cæsar briefly recapitulates the downward steps that have led him to his present condition. LAZARILLO, a poor, forlorn boy, who has just attempted to destroy himself, now attracts Don Cæsar's attention, and tells him the story of his wrongs. Don Cæsar becomes his friend, and is soon embroiled in a quarrel, which leads to a duel. Now, an edict has been passed, to punish with death all who engage in that mode of settling disputes, and Don Cæsar is arrested and conveyed to prison, while Don Jose promises Maritana an introduction to Court on the morrow.

At the commencement of the Second Act, we find Don Cæsar asleep in prison, while the boy Lazarillo watches near him. Don Cæsar is condemned to die at seven, and the hands of the clock point to five as he awakes: but two hours' life remain to him; yet he is gay, and ridicules all attempts to condole with him. Don Jose now enters, and, professing friendship for Don Cæsar, makes a proposition to him whereby his wish to die a soldier's death may be gratified on one condition—namely, that he shall marry! The alternative is to be hanged like a dog, or be married, and afterwards shot like a gentleman. For the last-named privilege, Don Cæsar consents to suffer matrimony for an hour and three-quarters. The Don assumes gay apparel for his wedding, and partakes of a banquet in honor of his nuptials. The preparations for his execution in military style proceed, but Lazarillo adroitly abstracts the messengers of death. At length, the hour arrives, and Don Cæsar is led forth to be shot, as the scene changes to a saloon in the Palace Montefiori, in which a festival is at its height. In the midst of the revelry, a volley of musketry is heard at a distance; this startles the guests, but the dance is soon resumed.

Don Jose, ever intent on the consummation of his deep-laid plans against the honor of the Queen, introduces Maritana to the MARQUIS and MARCHIONESS DE MONTEFIORI, and they, being his dependants, agree to present her to the King as their long-lost niece. The King makes warm and passionate professions to Maritana, and Don Jose promises to ensure their meeting at an appointed hour. As the King retires, Don Cæsar, disguised as a monk, joins the revellers, and claims of Don Cæsar as his bride. Don Jose is confounded, but, prompt in stratagems, he contrives to introduce the ugly old Marchioness to Don Cæsar as his wife! Of course, Don Jose is horror-struck! He repudiates her, but still believes himself deceived; and, hearing the voice of Maritana, he is confirmed in his belief. He becomes enraged, and demands his true wife. Don Jose orders his arrest, and that also of Maritana, and these two are borne away in different directions, as the Second Act ends.

The unhappy Maritana now pines in a villa belonging to the King, and Don Jose still secretly carries on his base designs against her honor, so that the King's infidelity may serve him as a stepping-stone to the Queen's favor. But Maritana is pure, and disregards all the King's proffers of wealth and luxury. Don Cæsar again arrives, at a fortunate moment, in search of his wife, and encountering the King, whom he does not recognize, a most amusing interview follows. The King is called away in haste, and Maritana and Don Cæsar meet, their love is mutual, and the plot of Don Jose is overthrown. His treason to the King, and intended villainy to the Queen, become apparent. Don Jose falls beneath Don Cæsar's sword. Don Cæsar secures his bride and an appointment as Governor of a distant city, beyond the reach of his creditors.

INDEX.

OVERTURE.

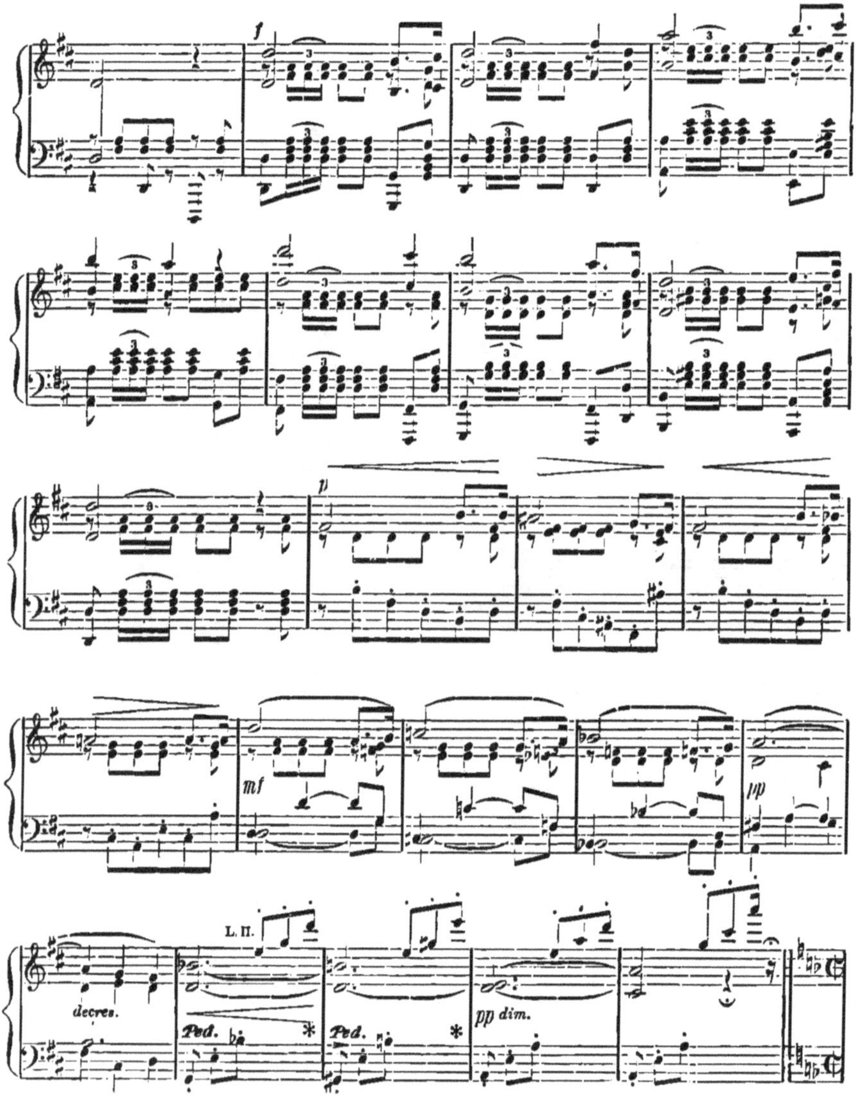
f
p
mf
pp
decres.
L. H.
Ped.
pp dim.

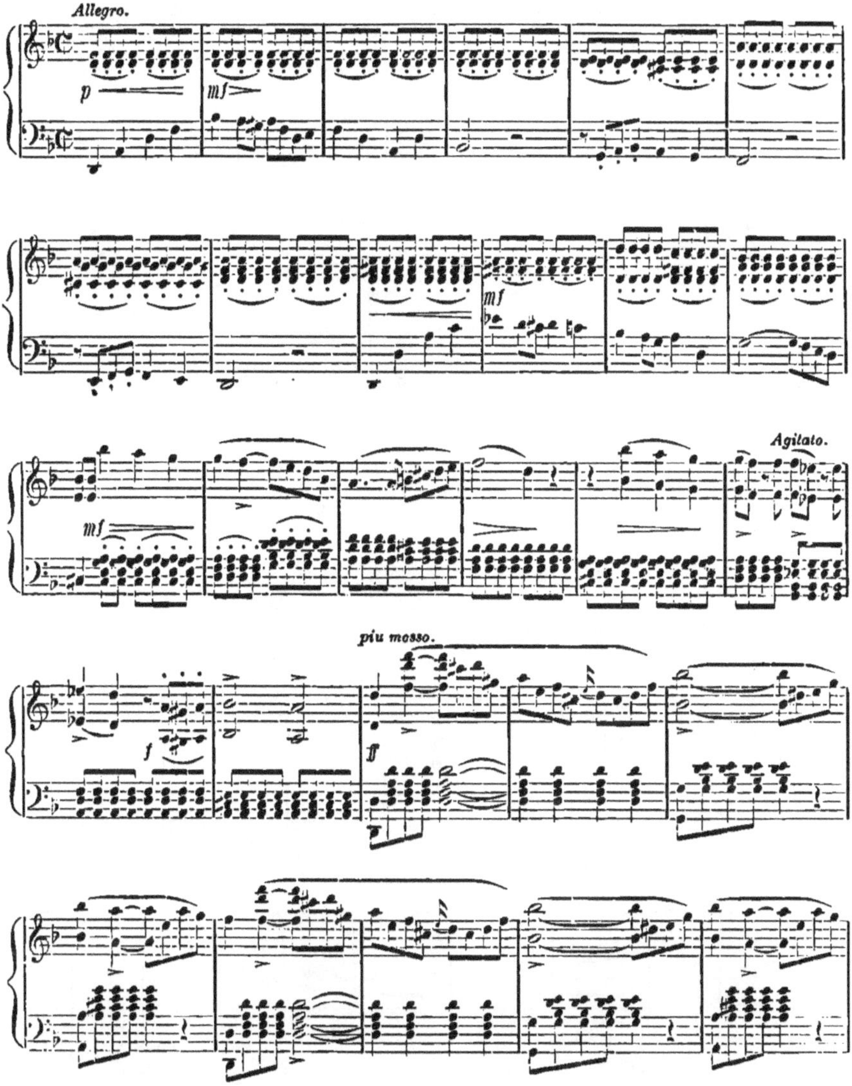
Allegro.
p
mf
mf
mf
Agitato.
piu mosso.
f
ff

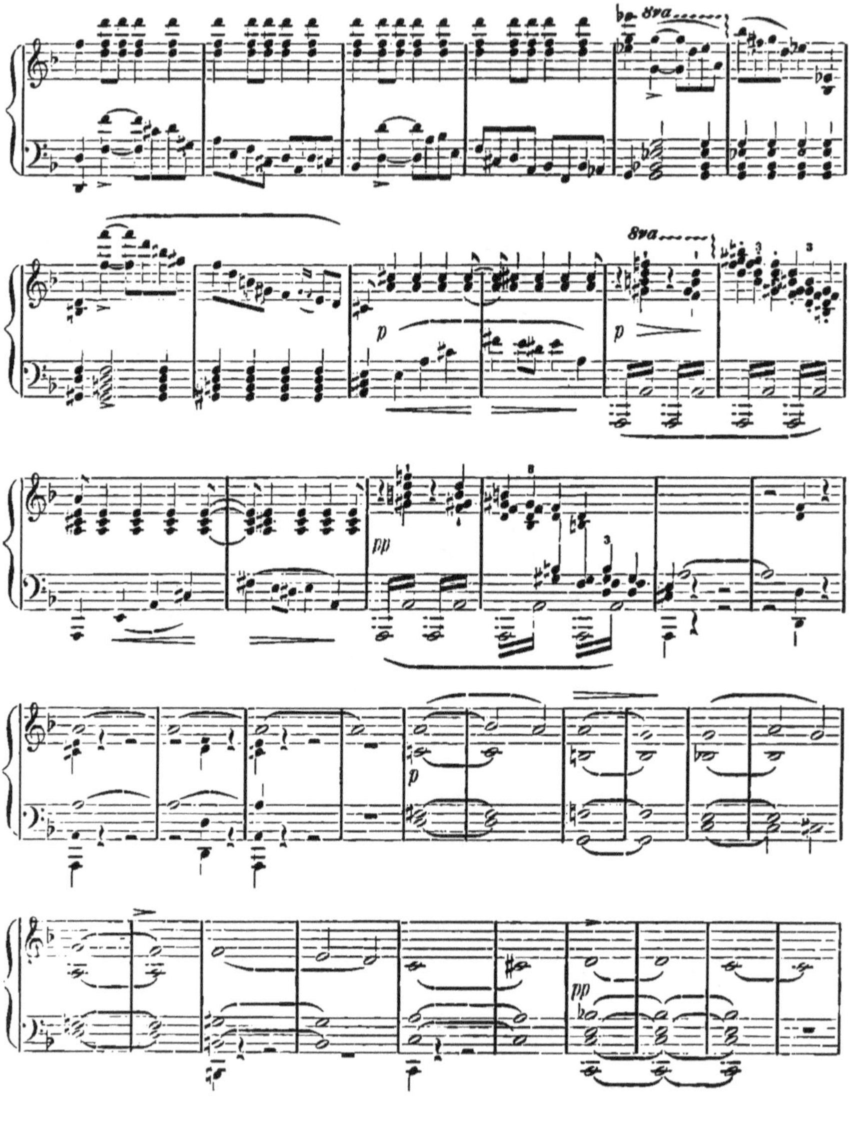
8va
p
pp

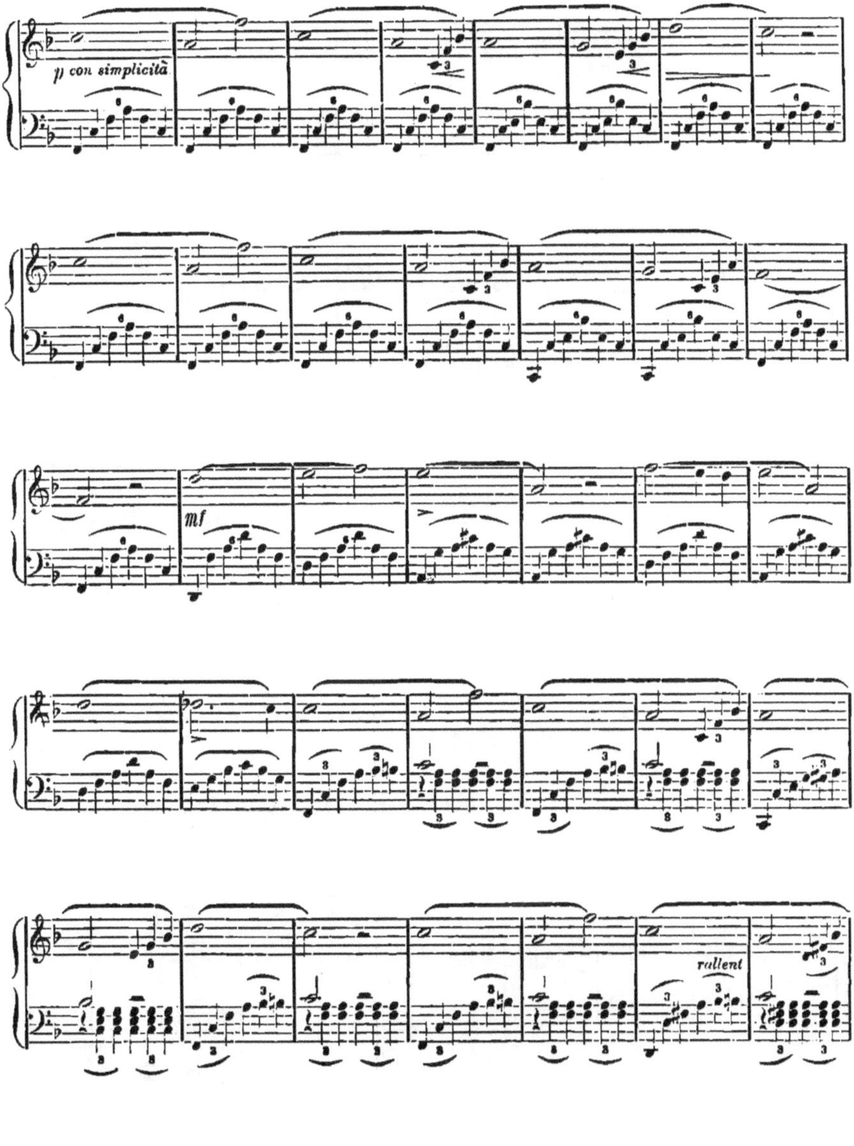
p con simplicità
mf
rallent

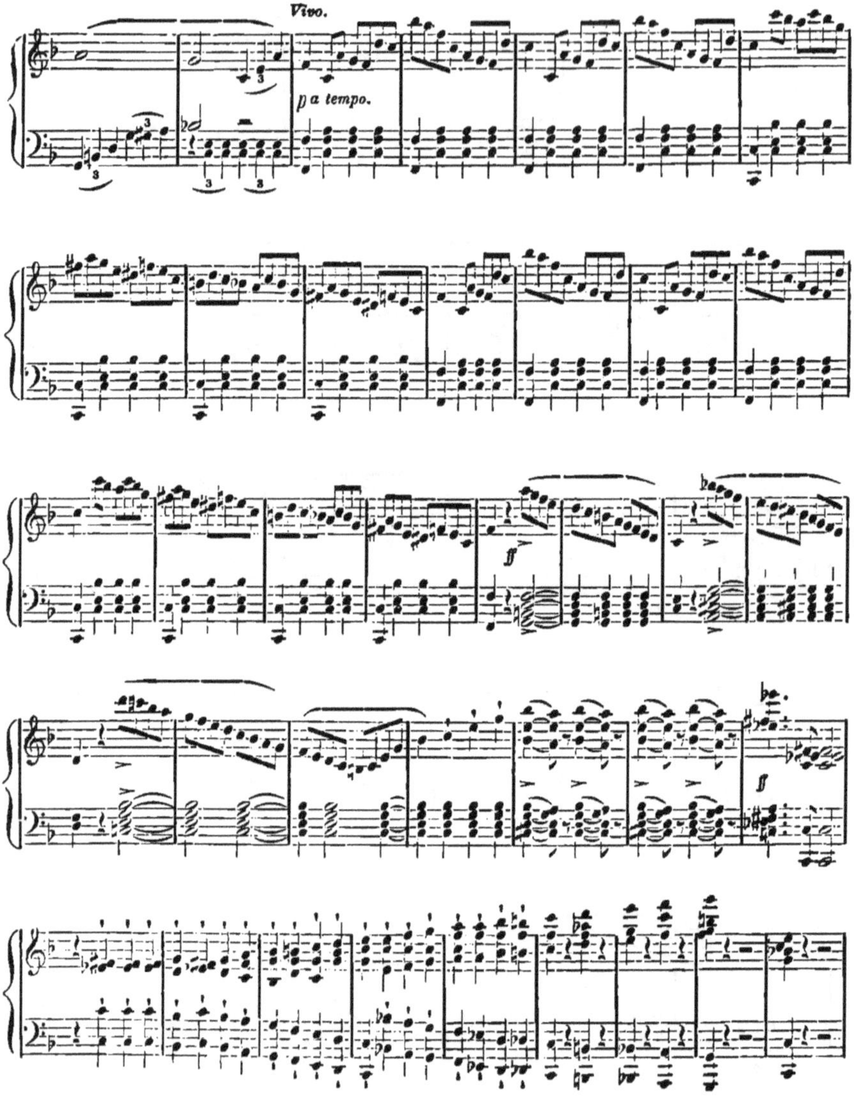
Vivo.
p a tempo.
ff
ff

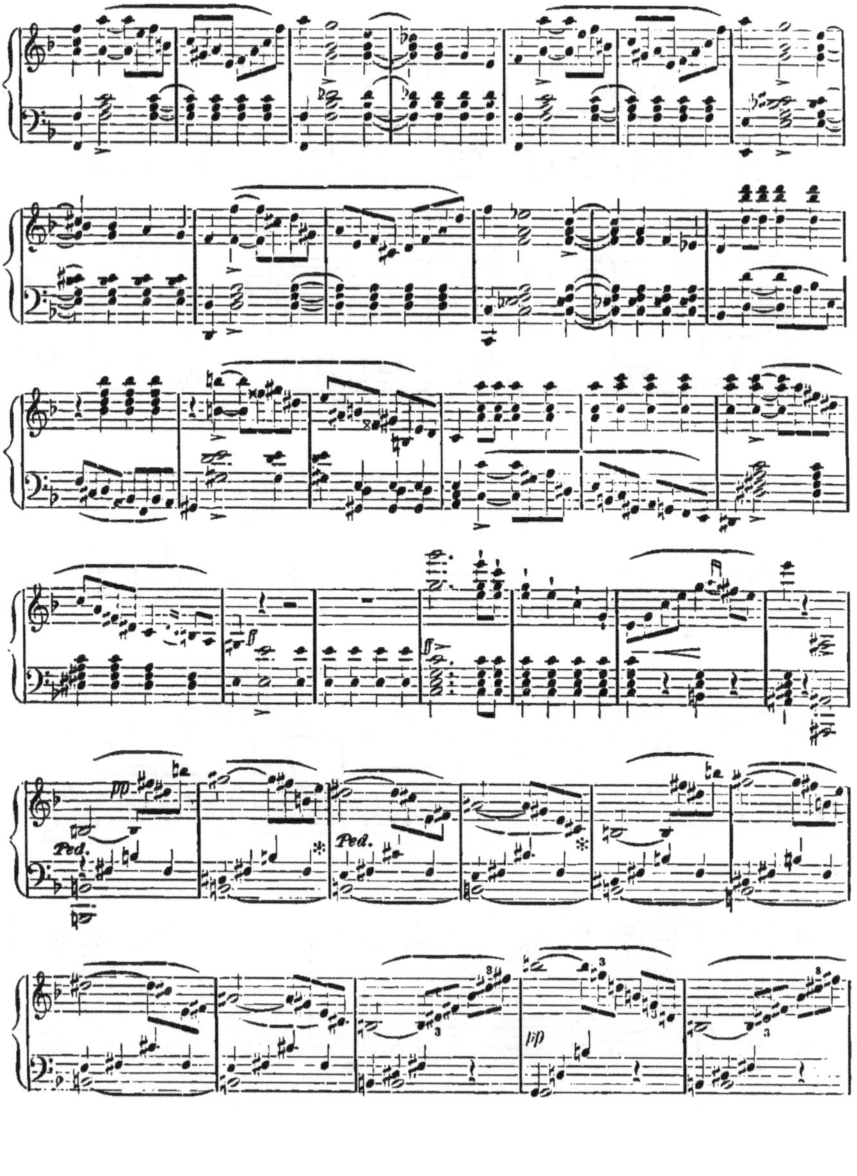
ff
pp
Ped.
Ped.
pp

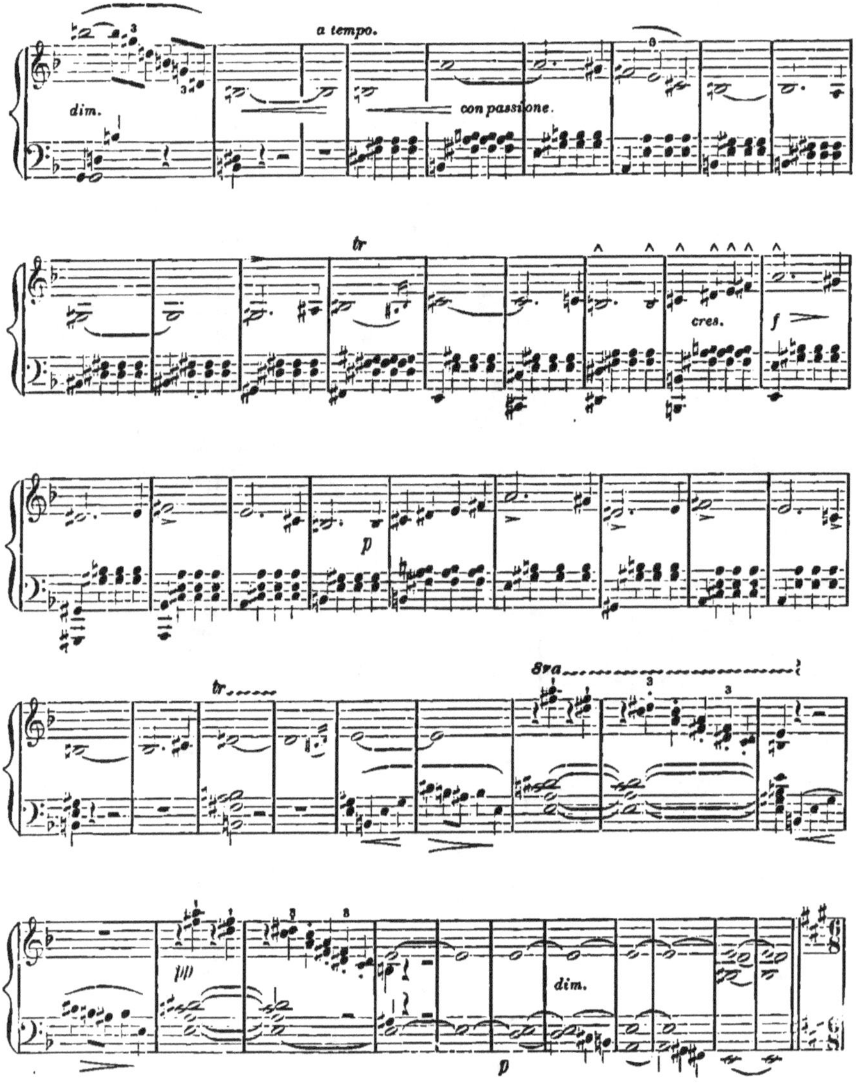
dim.
a tempo.
con passione.
tr
cres.
f
p
tr
8va
pp
dim.
p

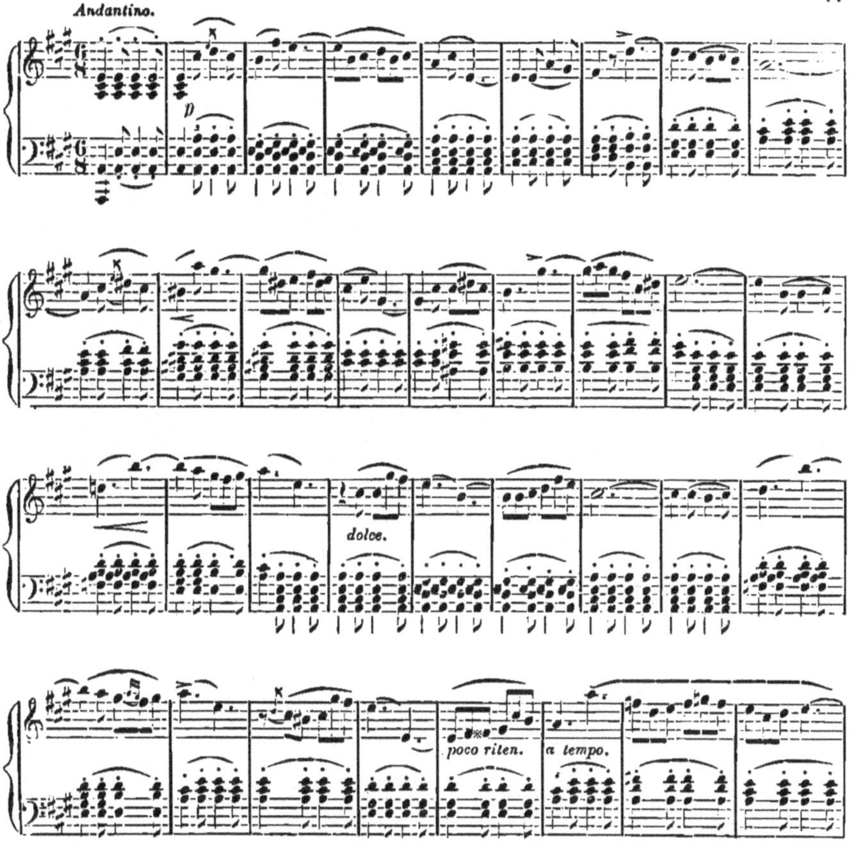
Andantino.
p
dolce.
poco riten.
a tempo.
decres.
pp

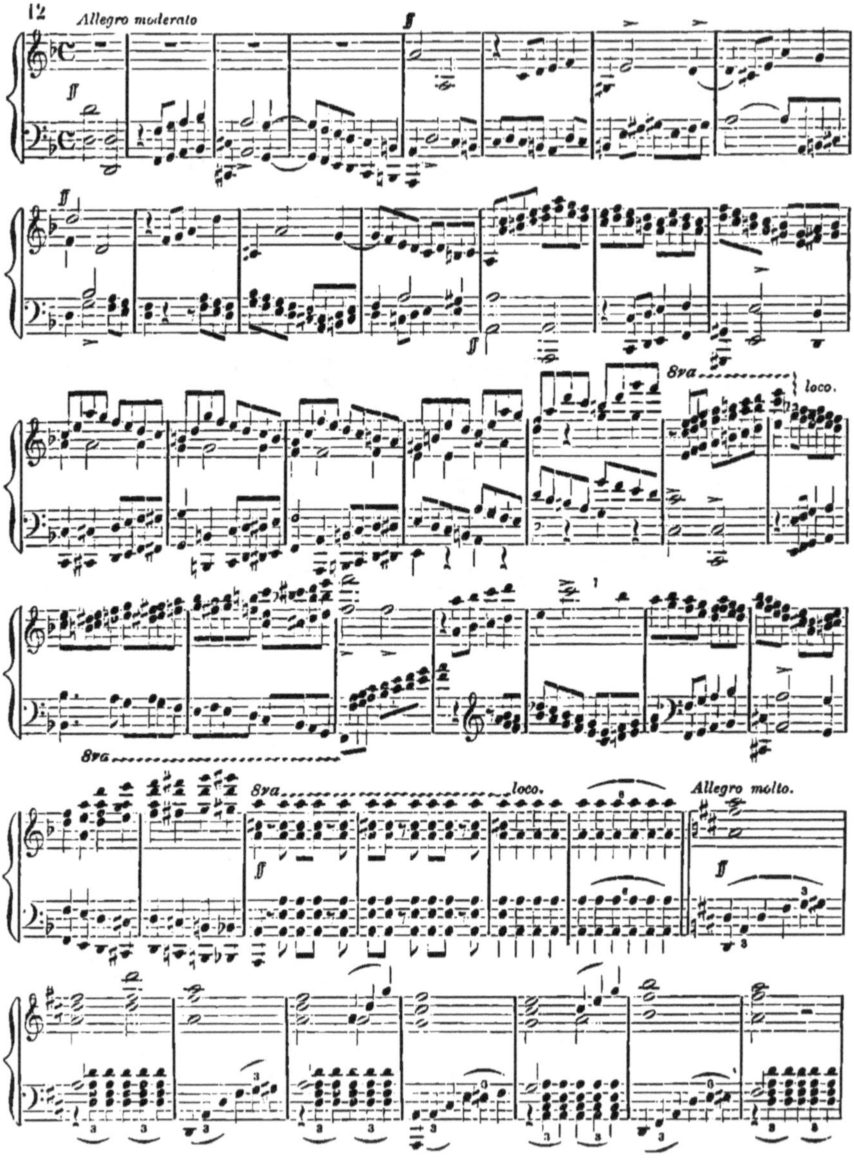
Allegro moderato
8va
loco.
8va
8va
loco.
Allegro molto.

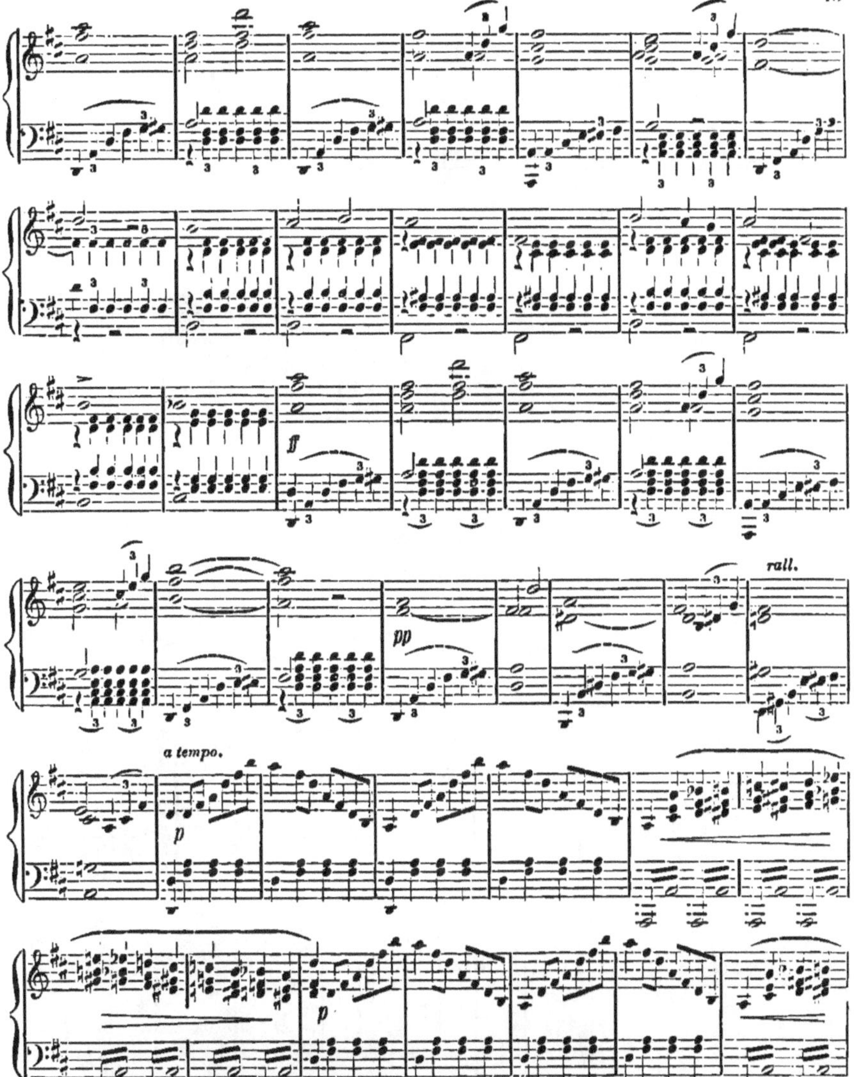
ff
pp
rall.
a tempo.
p
p

14

ACT I.

OPENING CHORUS.

No. 1.

A Square in Madrid.—Street F. *Set House* R. 2 E.—*People following* MARITANA, *who is singing.—The* KING *is among them disguised; appears to contemplate* MARITANA.

Sopranos.
Sing,.......... pret - ty maid - - en, sing,
Tenors.
Sing,.......... pret - ty maid - - en, sing,
Basses.
Sing,...... ... pret - ty maid - - en, sing, pret-ty maid - en
8va
ff
Sing,........ pret-ty maid - - en, sing, Sing that
Sing,........ pret-ty maid - - en, sing, Sing that
Sing,........ pret-ty naid - - en, sing, pret-ty maid - en Sing that
8va

love ly song, that love - ly song a - gain, Sing that
love ly song, that love ly song a - gain, pret - ty maid - -
love ly song, that love ly song a - gain, Sing that song........
song, that love - ly song a - gain, Sing that song, that
- - en, that love - ly song a - gain, Pret - ty maid - - en, that
that love - ly song a - gain, Sing that song........ that
8va

love - ly song a - gain, a - gain, a gain............

love - ly song a - gain, a - gain, a gain............

love - ly song a - gain, a - gain, a gain............

Sing, pret-ty maiden, The thrilling airs of Spain. Sing of love and beau-ty,

Sing, pret-ty maiden, The thrilling airs of Spain. Sing of love and beau-ty,

Sing, pret-ty maiden, The thrilling airs of Spain. Sing of love and beau-ty,

Bow'r or tent-ed plain.... Sing of love, sing of love, sing of love and beau-ty,

Bow'r or tent-ed plain.... Sing........ of love,...... sing of love and beau-ty,

Bow'r or tent-ed plain....Sing of love, sing of love, sing of love and beau-ty, sing of

20

plain, Pret-ty maiden, pret-ty maiden, Sing of love, sing of love and beau-ty,

plain, Pret ty maiden, pret-ty maiden, Sing of love and beauty, Pret-ty

plain, Pret-ty maiden, pret-ty maiden, Sing of love and beauty, Pret-ty

Sing of love and of beau-ty, Bow'r or tent - ed plain, of Spain, of

maiden, pret-ty maiden, sing the thrill-ing.... airs of Spain, of Spain, of

maiden, pret-ty maiden, sing the thrill-ing.... airs of Spain, of Spain, of

Spain, the thrill-ing airs, the thrill-ing airs of Spain, of Spain, Sing of

Spain, the thrill-ing airs, the thrill-ing airs of Spain, of Spain, Sing of

Spain, Pretty maid en, sing,..... the thrill-ing airs..... of Spain,.... of Spain, Sing of

love, sing of love and beauty, sing of love and beauty, Bow'r or tent ed

love, sing of love and beauty, sing of love and beauty, Bow'r or tent-ed

love, sing of love and beauty, sing of love and beauty, Bow'r or tent-ed plain, Sing of love and beau - - ty, Bow'r or tent - ed

plain, Sing of love and beau - - ty, Bow'r or tent - ed

plain, Sing of love and beau - - ty, Bow'r or tent - ed

plain, Sing, sweet Ma - ri - ta - - na, sing that song a -

plain, Sing, sweet Ma - ri - ta - - na, sing that song a -

plain, Sing, sweet Ma - ri - ta - - na, sing that song a -

- gain, sing of love and beau - - ty, Bow'r or ten - ted
- gain, sing of love and beau - - ty, Bow'r or ten - ted
- gain, sing of love and beau - - ty, Bow'r or ten - ted
8va
plain, Sing, sweet Ma - ri - ta - - na, sing that song a -
plain, Sing, sweet Ma - ri - ta - - na, sing that song a -
plain, Sing, sweet Ma - ri - ta - - na, sing that song a -
8va

gain, sing, Gi - ta - - na, sing, sing, Gi ta - - na,

gain, sing, Gi - ta - na, sing, sing, Gi - ta - na,

gain, sing, Gi - ta - - na, sing, sing, Gi - ta na,

sing, sing that song a - gain, that song a - gain........

sing, sing that song a - gain, that song a - gain........

sing, sing that song a - gain, that song a - gain........

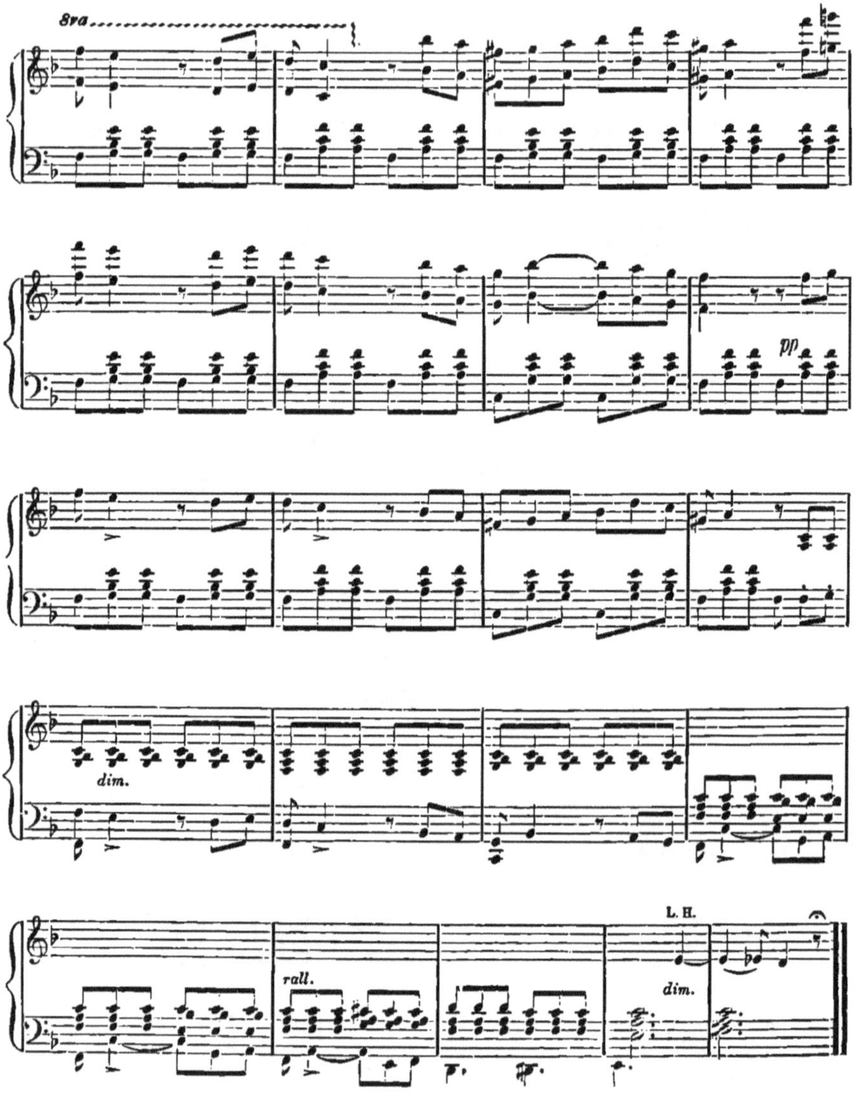
8va
pp
dim.
rall.
L. H.
dim.

"IT WAS A KNIGHT."

No. 2.

ROMANCE.

Scherzando.

MARITANA.

It was a Knight of princely mien, One blue and gold-en day.

Came ri - ding thro' the for - est green, That round his castle lay.

And there heard he a Gip-sy maid, her

song of love re-veal, And there heard he, a Gip-sy maid, her

song of love re-veal, And there heard he a Gip-sy maid, her

song of love re-veal........

Like a spir - it, a spir - it of light,

She en - chant - ed, en- chant - ed the Knight, 'Twas a

CHORUS. MARITANA.

King, 'Twas a King, 'twas the King, 'twas the King of Cas - tille,

CHORUS.

Sing, sing Ma-ri-ta na, no de-lay, no de - lay, Love's
min - strel Ma - ri - ta - na, we will pay, thus we
pay, thus we pay, thus we pay.
(Giving her money.)
8va
loco.
Ped.

MARITANA.

Her beau - ty's blaze, her magic tone, His lost heart fled in

vain. And

soon he rais'd her to a throne, O'er fair Cas-tillo to reign.

And so it chanc'd a Gip-sy maid, As

le-gends old...... . re - veal,   And so   it chanc'd a   Gip - sy maid,   As

le   gends old re- veal,   And so   it chanc'd a Gip - sy maid,   As

le   gends old re - veal..

Like a spir - it, a spir - - it of light,

For en chant - ing, en-chant - ing a Knight, Was a

CHORUS.   MARITANA.

Queen, Was a Queen, Was a Queen, was a Queen of Cas- tille.

34

CHORUS.

Sing, sing Ma - ri - ta na, no de - lay, no de - lay, Love's

min - strel Ma - ri - ta - na, we will pay, thus we

pay, thus we pay, thus we pay.

KING. (*with passion.*) How beautiful she is !
(*Enter* DON JOSE, R. U. E.)
DON JOSE. (*advancing*) He ! It is the third time I have discovered him on this spot.
MARITANA. (*to the* KING.) Good signor, haven't you a single maravedi at the bottom of your purse ? It might better require a poor singer than those forlorn looks. (*The* KING *gives her money, then exits hastily.* L. 2. E.) A quadruple of gold! I can scarcely believe I am not dreaming again.
DON JOSE. You have received a good offering this morning, eh, my little syren ?
MARITANA. Yes, a golden quadruple! He must be some very rich man !
DON JOSE. Very ; Don Arias Count of Fuentes, the most opulent gentleman in Spain. (*Aside.*) Your Majesty's secret is worth possessing. I shall improve my acquaintance with this handsome Gitana; her star is in the ascendant. (*Aloud.*)

So, my little mountain fairy, what song will you sing me, for the fellow to that golden piece, which glitters still in your pretty hand !
MARITANA. Sing ? Anything, signor—what shall it be ?
DON JOSE. Let me recollect. Oh, the legend which you warbled to the Queen yesterday ; her Majesty stopped her carriage to listen to you, I was told
MARITANA. That is no more than truth, signor.
DON JOSE. It must have been an interesting ditty.
MARITANA. A mere romance, popular in Madrid, said often to have been heard at midnight, in some old ruined palace of the Moorish kings, far over the mountains yonder ;— they call it the "Harp in the air."
DON JOSE. By all means, sing it.
MARITANA. Willingly, signor,—but I must first summon my attendant spirits. (*Beckoning forward the* GIPSIES *for chorus.*

'TIS THE HARP IN THE AIR.

No. 3.   Maritana.

pp   una corda.   Ped.   *

8va   8va

Ped.   *   Ped.   pp   *

MARITANA.

I bear it a-gain!........ ....   'Tis the Harp!............. ...
8va

....   'tis the Harp.....................   in   the   air,...........
8va   8va

Ped.   *

Ped.   *

36

It hangs on the walls........ ... of the old moor-ish

halls,........... It hangs on the walls........... of the old moor-ish

halls,........... Tho' none.. .... know its min - - strel, or

how it came there,................ Listen! Listen!

a piacere.

mf

Ped. *p* *pp* *※*

Ped. *※*

There! There!......................

'Tis the harp in the air,.... ... .
'Tis the Harp!...........

'tis the harp............ ...8va.....
in the air,...........

It

tell - eth of days .... that are fad - - ed and gone, ... It tell - eth of the brave, of the
dim.
love - ly and fair, ... Of war - - rior's grave, and of maid - - en's de - spair.
8va
pp
Ped.
There, there,
8va
pp una corda.
Ped.
*
Ped.
*
there, ... there, ...
8va
Ped.
*
p
Ped.
*

List, Pil - grim, list, ... 'tis the harp in the air,........ List, Pil - grim,

pp tre corde.

Ped.

cres.

list,.... 'tis the harp in the air, ... List, Pil - grim, list,... 'tis the

Ped.

Ped.

cres.

harp in the air, ... List, Pil - grim, list,.... 'tis the harp in the

Ped.

air,............ List, Pil - grim, list..... 'tis the harp in the air,........

una corda.

cres.

Ped.

DON JOSE. Brava! brava! take the recompense your sweet song richly deserves.
MARITANA. Another golden quadruple! See, friends, I shall be affluent indeed! Oh, thanks, thanks, signor! (*Chimes heard.*)
Ah! the Angelus! Such good fortune should admonish us to be doubly devout! (*They kneel.*)

"ANGELS THAT AROUND US HOVER."

No. 4. ANGELUS.

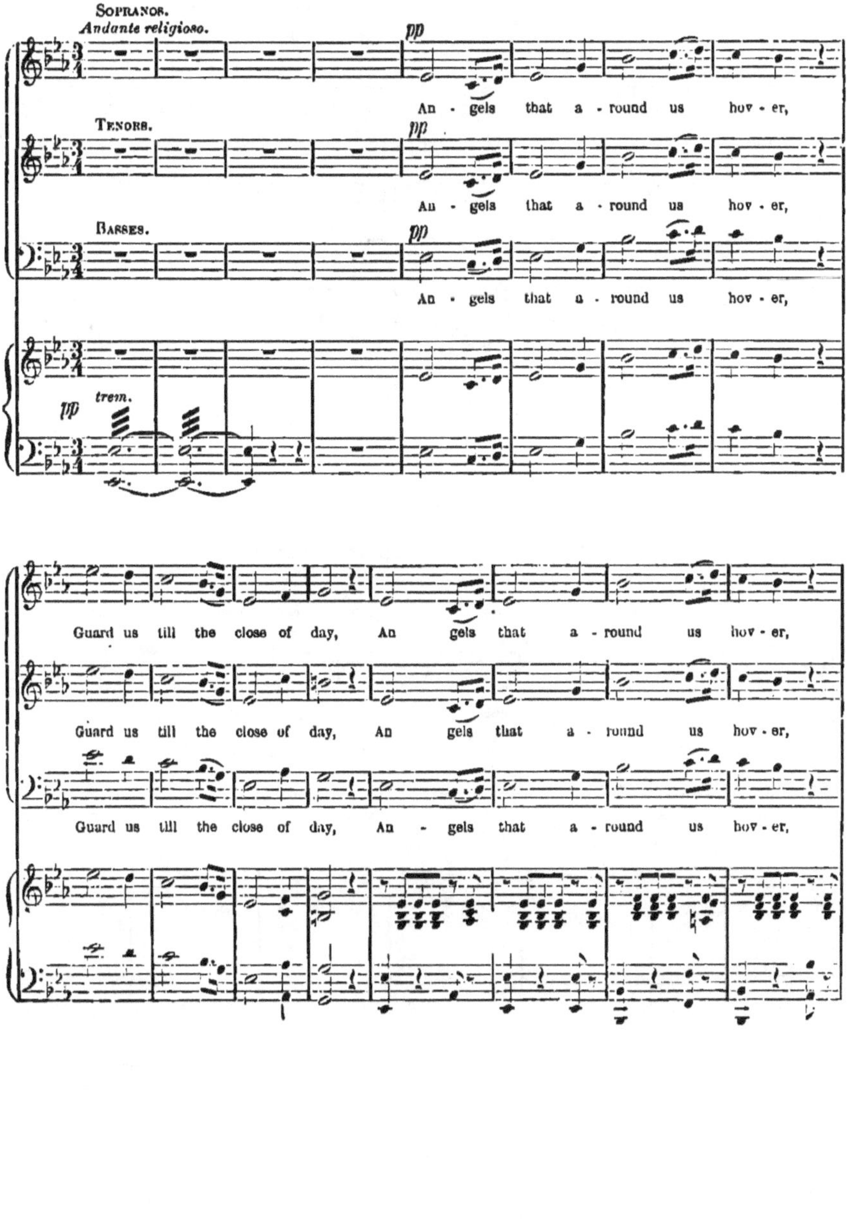

Guard us till the close of day Our heads, oh! let your

Guard us till the close of day. Our heads, oh! let your

Guard us till the close of day. Our heads, oh! let your

white wings cov - er, See us kneel, and hear us pray, See us

white wings cov - er, See us kneel, and hear us pray, See us

white wings cov - er, See us kneel, and hear us pray, See us kneel, and hear us pray,...... An - - gels that a - round us

kneel, and hear us pray,........ An gels that a - round us

kneel, and hear us pray,........ An - - gels that a - round us

hov - er, Guard us till the close of day. Our heads, oh!

bov - er, Guard us till the close of day. Our heads, oh!

bov - er, Guard us till the close of day. Our heads, oh!

let your white wings cov - er, See us kneel, and hear us
let your white wings cov - er, See us kneel, and hear us
p
let your white wings cov - er, See us kneel, and hear us
cres.
ff
cres.
ff
pp
pray, See.... us kneel, and hear us pray, See.... us
pp
pray, See.... us kneel, and hear us pray, See.... us
pp
pray, See us kneel, See us kneel, and hear us pray, See.... us
pp

pp
kneel, and hear us pray, Hear us
pp
kneel, and hear us pray, Hear us
pp
hear us pray, Hear us
pp
ff
pray, hear us pray, See us kneel, and hear
ff
pray, hear us pray, See us kneel, and hear
ff
pray, hear us pray, See us kneel, and hear
ff

us pray, and hear us pray..........

us pray, and hear us pray.........

us pray, and hear us pray..........

f
fff

(*All exeunt except* MARITANA, *who remains still on her knees, looking at the piece of gold in her lap.*)

DON JOSE. Why do you sigh in contemplating your gains?

MARITANA. Because they are still too little, or too much, Signor.

DON JOSE. What mean you?

MARITANA. Too much for remunerating songs of a poor Gitana, and too little to confirm the dreams of splendor which nightly occupy my slumbers.

DON JOSE. Ah! a Gitana, then, has her dreams of greatness.

MARITANA. Yes, I fancy myself in a gilded coach, glittering with jewels! Oh, I despair of such visionary promises ever coming to pass! I—feathers—diamonds—Ha! ha! ha!

OF FAIRY WAND HAD I THE POWER.

No. 5. DUET. Maritana and Don Jose.

Allegro non troppo.

p

MARITANA.

Of fai - ry wand had I the power, Some palace bright my home should be.

RECIT.

p

By marble fount, in orange bower, Dancing to music's me - lo - dy.

DON JOSE.
a tempo.

Those lovely eyes, those ruby lips, Might win a bright- er home for

p

48

thee, Than crys - - tal ball, where Fai - - ry trips light - ly, to

ech - o's, to ech- o's minstrel- sy.

Allegro Moderato.

MARITANA.

Of Fai - ry wand had I........ com - mand,

At moon-lit hour, in silk - - en bow'r, To music's note, on

air, on air I'd float, To mu - sic's note on air I'd float, on

air, on air I'd float, In golden sheen, And jewels gay, Of pleasure, Queen, of pleasure,

Queen, I'd laugh and sing, and dance and play,... I'd laugh and

50

sing,   and dance, and play...................................... of pleas - ure, Queen,   I'd laugh and

sing, and dance, and play, of pleas - ure, Queen,   I'd dance, and sing.... and........ play,........   and

play.

DON JOSE.

Those sparkling eyes.......... are brighter prize,

Than gems that glow on King - - ly brow of those a -
- vail, ere yet they fade, of those a - vail, ere
yet they fade, ere yet, ere yet they fade, For joy will quail when time o'er-shade, For joy will
quail .... when time o'er-shade, then laugh while love ... and beauty aid, ... then laugh while love and beauty
p

aid,   then laugh while love.... and beauty aid,.......... while love and beau - ty aid, then laugh while

love,   then laugh while love and beau - - ty aid, then laugh while love, while love and

beau . . . . ty aid.

Violoncello.

Larghetto

pp   *dim.*

MARITANA. (*Aside.*)

He thinks as oth - ers oft have done, My wild fan - tas - - tic

thoughts are vain, Are vis - - ions all, now here, now gone Like dreams that rise and fade a -

51

DON JOSÉ. (*Aside.*)

- gain.　Thus! woman's heart .... is ev - er bought;　Gold brightly gleam.... but in her

eyes.　So,　by the flame, the moth is　caught.　Burneth its gid - dy wing, and

cres.

MARITANA.

dies.　He　thinks,　as oth - ers　oft　have done, My wild fan - tas - - tic thoughts are vain, Are vis - - ions all, now here, now gone Like dreams that rise and fade a -

MARITANA.

\- gain. Are vis - ions all, now here, now

DON JOSE.

Thus .... woman's heart is ev - er bought,............ .... woman's heart is ev - er

gone Like...... dreams, like...... dreams that........ rise and fade, ... and fade a-

bought, Gold bright - ly gleam but in her eyes, Gold bright-ly ... gleam ...... but in her

56

Allegro.   DON JOSÉ.

p

Think of the

splen - - dor, the golden glo - - ry, the bright ca - - reer.... which

waits your fu - - ture steps; One round of

f

MARITANA.

tri - - - - - - - umph.   Or

ff

Fai - - ry wand had I........ com - mand, Of Fai - - ry wand had

pp

I.... com - mand, At moon - - lit hour in sil - - ken bow - er To mu - - sic's

note, on air I'd float,.... To mu - - sic's note on air I'd float.

f

DON JOSE.

Those spark - ling eyes are bright - - er prize Than gems that glow on

p

king - - ly brow; Of those a - vail, ere yet .... they fade, For joy will

quail when time o'er - shade..... Then laugh while love and beau - - ty

MARITANA.

In gold - - en sheen and jew - - els gay, Of pleas - - ure's Queen I'd

DON JOSE.

aid. Those spark - - ling eyes are bright - - er prize Than gems that glow on

60

laugh and sing, In gold - - en sheen and jew - - els gay, Of pleas - - ure's

King - - ly brow; Of those a - vail, ere yet .... they fade, For joy will

Queen, I'd laugh and sing, Of pleas - - ure's Queen I'd laugh and sing.

quall, when time o'er - shade, Then laugh while love and beau - - ty aid.

Of pleas - ure's Queen

Then laugh while love

cres - - - - - - cen -

p

I'd laugh and sing. Of pleas - ure's Queen,

and beau - ty aid. Then laugh while love

- - - - - do.

I'd laugh and sing, Of pleas - - - ure's

and beau - ty aid. Then laugh while

Queen I'd laugh and sing, and sing............ Ah! Of

love, while love and beau - - ty aid............ Those

62

Of .... pleas - ure's Queen .... I'd laugh, ... I'd
pp
laugh .... and sing. Of.... ... pleas - ure's Queen .... I'd
Then laugh, then laugh while love,
dance .... and play, ... I'd dance and .... play, I'd dance and
Then laugh while love and beau - - ty aid, Then laugh while

64

play, I'd dance and play, I'd dance and sing.

love and beau - - ty aid, and beau - - ty aid.

Don Jose. (*aside.*) The vain little coquette.

Maritana. You laugh at my folly, signor ?

D. Jose. Not in the least: what better, to command wealth than such a passport of beauty ?

Mar. Ah, signor, now indeed, I know you are jesting with me ! [*Cry without of " the* Queen ! "

Mar. Listen ! There's the Queen passing through the grand square. If I could only attract her notice again ! Adieu, signor, ambitious as I am, I can still remember to be grateful.

[*Exit* R. U. E. *singing* " Of fairy wand," &c.

D. Jose. Au revoir, ma belle Maritana ! Yes, yes, your aspiring dreams will come to pass, since, through your influence over the heart of the King, Don Jose looks to realize his own over that of the neglected Queen. Once persuaded of her husband's infidelity, might not the incensed wife be induced to look, even from her throne, for an object worthy of assisting her just revenge ! Then, Don Jose — yes, yes, Maritana, your dreams *will* come to pass, and speedily ! (*Noise.*) Ah ! whom have we here ?

[*Enter* Don Cæsar, *from* D. *Hotel of somewhat humble description,* R. 2. E. *evidently a little inebriated.*]

Don Cæsar. Miserable knaves ! why, they cheat at cards without conscience, as if they were privileged, like our nobles of Madrid. Oh, if it were no dishonor to my sword to chastise such canaille ! Robbed, plundered of my last maravedi ! I shall sup on cold air to-night, and sleep—where I shall have the whole blue expanse above for my bed curtains !—ha ! ha ! ha !

D. Jose. Am I mistaken ? No, it is Don Cæsar de Bazan !

D. Cæsar. Don Jose de Santarem ?

D. Jose. The same. It is long since we met, Don Cæsar ; you have been sometime absent from Madrid ?

D. Cæsar. On my travels.

D. Jose. They say travel changes a man. (*Regarding him.*)

D. Cæsar. And his apparel ? (*Laughing.*) Ha ! ha ! ha !

D. Jose. Your noble father left you a high name, and a brilliant inheritance.

D. Cæsar. The name I still bear : the inheritance benefits mankind.

D. Jose. You had numerous followers !

D. Cæsar. So I have still—*creditors !* Go where I may, *they* are *sure* to follow me ; and, as I am very fond of change, by my valor, but I give them some trouble to run after me. Ha ! ha ! ha !

No. 6.

Allegro ma non troppo.

D. CAESAR.

All the world o - ver, all the world o - ver, To love, to drink, to

fight I de - light, All the world o - ver I de - light, To love, to drink, to fight I de- light.

ad lib.

colla voce

66

Drink with the Fa - ther, Woo with the Daugh- ter, woo with the Daugh- ter,

Fight with the lov - er, Wing'd like the swal - low where spring flow'rs in -

- vite............ Wing'd like the swal - low where spring flow'rs in -

dol.

- vite, By changing the scene, All, all is se-rene, by changing the scene, All, all is se - rene,.......... And skies

a piacre.

calm - ly blue............... Bright, bright as the dew............ ....And

skies calm - ly blue,........... For me,.... for me, ev - er shine........

And skies ev - er blue; ...... for me, ev - er shine.. .... for me ev - er shine........... I'm al - - ways re - sign'd........... Wher-ev - er I find...........

War, beauty or wine war, beauty or
wine, I'm al - ways re - sign'd, wher-ev er I
find, War, beau - ty or wine, war, beauty or
wine, Wher - e - ver I find, wher - e - ver I find, War, beau - ty or
p
8va
cres.
ff

wine, I'm al - ways re- sign'd, wher-ev er I
p
find, War, beau- ty or wine, war, beauty or
8va
cres.
wine, Wher- e - ver I find, wher- e - ver I find, War, beau - ty or
ff
wine.............. .... war, beau- ty or wine..........................
8va
ff
p
ff

war, beau-ty or wine, war, beauty or wine, war,

beauty or wine...........

D. JOSE. (L.) And what happy event has restored you to your native city?

D. CAESAR. [R.] Hope! the rainbow hope! that my creditors were all dead! Alas! creditors, like the imperishable laurel, never die! But, tell me, what news here? drink they the same, and fight as many duels as formerly?

D JOSE. Duels have become rare in Madrid since the edict of the king.

D. CAESAR. What edict?

D. JOSE. One which declares that all who fight with the sword, shall be shot; except during Holy-week, and then the survivor is condemned to be—

D. CAESAR. What?

D. JOSE. Hanged.

D. CAESAR. Um! If I mistake not, Holy-week commenced today.

D. JOSE. Exactly so.

D. CAESAR. Then, I must keep out of a passion. Hanged! I shouldn't survive the disgrace. (Noise without.) Ha! ha! ha! What is all this?

[Enter LAZARILLO and BOATMAN. L. U. E.]

BOATMAN. Foolish boy! I insist on conducting you to your friends.

LAZ. [R.] Why did you prevent me from drowning myself? I wish to die.

D. CAESAR. [C.] Eh! Die at your age? Drown yourself? You cannot have many creditors, surely?

LAZ. No, signor; but I am apprenticed to a stern master—an armorer—who, under pretence that the corslets were not kept bright, beat me again today.

D. CAESAR. Again! Hath he beaten thee ere now?

LAZ. Yes, signor, frequently; 'till I can no longer endure it. I prefer death! (Terrified. Crossing to L. U. E.) Ah, they come to arrest me-

D. CAESAR. (opposing himself.) Fear nothing. I'll interpose

LAZ. Alas! that captain will not hear of pity.

D. CAESAR. I shall defend you with my sword. (Touching his sword hilt.)

D. JOSE. [L.] (putting his hand on his arm.) Recollect! Holy-week!

[CAPTAIN and SOLDIERS enter, together with citizens. LAZ. (R.) DON C. (R. C.) DON. J. (C.) CAPT. (L. C.) GUARDS. (L.)

"SEE THE CULPRIT."

No. 7.

Allegro vivo.

CAPTAIN. LAZARILLO. CAPTAIN. LAZARILLO. CAPTAIN.

See the culprit. Mer - cy, mer - cy. Quick, ar - rest him. Mer - cy, mer-cy. See the

cul - prit, quick, ar - rest him, See the cul - prit, quick, ar - rest him, See the cul - prit,

quick, ar - rest him, See the cul - prit, quick, ar - rest him! Why my orders dis - o - bey you, Why my

Lazarillo.
or-ders dis-o - bey you, Why my orders dis - o - bey, Why my orders dis - o - bey?
Mer - cy, mer - cy.
D. Cæsar.
List I pray you,
Lazarillo.
Mer - cy, mer - cy,
D. Cæsar.
List, I pray you! If a mere child's
poor en - treaty, Fail to move that heart of thine, If his voice ex -
- cite no pi - ty, Bro - ther sol - diers, list to mine.
Captain.
Come, your du - ty quick - ly

D. CÆSAR.

Oh! if 'twere not ho - ly week, Oh! if 'twere not ho - ly

CAPTAIN.

seek. Come, your du - ty quick - ly seek.

week, Him I'd send soon to the dev - il. Oh! if

pray'rs and tears won't make me civ - il. Come, your du - ty quick-ly seek.

'twere not ho - ly week! Oh! if 'twere not ho - ly week!

Come, your du - ty quickly seek. Come,

Oh ! if 'twere not ho - ly week ! Him I'd send soon to the dev - il. Gallant

come, your du - ty quickly seek, pray'rs and tears wont make me civ - il.

Cap - tain !

Gallant Captain !

Loose my cloak.

Loose my

ff

Rage consumes me ! I shall choke, rage consumes me ! I shall choke, rage consumes me! I shall choke.

cloak.

rall.

a tempo

LAZARILLO.

Mer - cy, mercy!   mer - cy, mercy!

D. CÆSAR.

Oh! if 'twere not holy week   out his cursed brains I'll

CAPTAIN.

Come, your du - ty seek....   Come, your du - ty seek....

p

Stay   this   cru - el   an - ger, stay,   Pi - ty   and   for - give - ness, pray.

dash.

quick   if   you'd   es-cape   the   lash.   quick   if   you'd   es - cape   the   lash.

LAZARILLO.

Ne'er a - gain will I be rash. Pi - ty, and with - hold the lash.

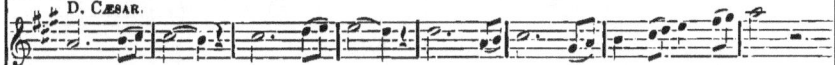

D. CÆSAR.

Out his cur - sed brains I'll dash, Out his curs - ed brains, his brains I'll dash.

D. JOSE.

With the churl do not be rash, With the churl do not be rash.

D. CÆSAR.

Must I this scorn? One word! men, I vengeance, in - stant

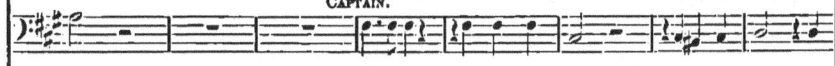

CAPTAIN.

March! Mendicant, be not ab - surd, be not ab - surd, be

D. JOSE.

78

ven - geance, in - stant ven - geance wreak. Oh! if it were not

not ab - surd, be not ab - surd, Thou threat'nest in - so - lent?

D. JOSE.
With the churl do not be rash.

LAZARILLO.
Stay this cru - el an - ger, stay this cru - el

D. CÆSAR.
ho - ly - week. Be - ware! Still to pro - voke me do not dare, still to pro-

CAPTAIN.
In - so - lent, be - ware, beware,hence,miscreant

D. JOSE.
With the churl do not be rash, with the churl do not be rash, do not be

an - ger stay, this cru - el an - ger stay,.... Pi - ty and for -
- voke me do not dare, still to pro - voke me do not dare,
fly hence, miscreant, fly hence, miscreant, fly hence, miscreant, hence,
rash, do not be rash, do not be rash, do not be rash,
scen - - - - - - do.
ff
8va
- give - - ness, and for - give - - ness pray, Ne'er a
to pro - voke me do not dare, still to pro-
mis - - creant, fly, mis - creant, fly hence, miscreant,
with the churl do not be rash, do not be
p cre - - -

- gain will I be rash, ne'er a - gain will I be rash,

-voke me do not dare, still to pro - voke me do not dare,

fly hence, miscreant, fly hence, miscreant, fly hence, miscreant, hence,

rash, do not be rash, do not be rash, do not be rash,

scen - - - - - do.

pi - - ty, and with - hold the lash, with - hold the

(Grasping sword.)

to pro - voke me do not dare, or on the

mis - - creant, fly, hence mis - creant, fly hence, miscreant,

do not be rash, do not be

lash, with-hold the lash, with-hold the lash, with-hold the lash.

spot, great Cap-tain, I'll kill thee out-right, kill thee out-right.

fly hence, miscreant, fly hence, miscreant, fly hence, miscreant fly!

rash, do not be rash, do not be rash, do not be rash.

D. CÆSAR. (*Proudly, with dignity.*)

Know, Sir, Who I am! Count of Ga-ro-fa! Don Cæ-sar de Ba-zan! Who in the

ad lib. f

presence, in the presence of his Monarch, Covered hath a right, hath a

right to ap - pear. You have in - sulted me be -

- yond all bearing; Redress I seek! re-dress I seek! Hence to the de-vil with the holy

(Draws sword.)

(Strikes him with his sword.) CAPTAIN.

week! redress I seek! redress I seek! thus I chas-tise, chastise such daring. A

Cap. a piacere.
(Draws.)
D. Cæsar.
a piacere.
chal - lenge! ven - geance, A chal - lenge! for - ward.
Chorus.
A chal - lenge! the E - dict! hor - ror!
Allegro vivace.
Lazarillo.
Oh for - bear! in - deed you must.... Be this fright - ful
D. Cæsar.
Oh, you soon shall bite the dust.... Hon - or's debt is
Captain.
Come, you will not prove the first Brag - gart whom this
D. Jose.
Don't for - get be - fore you thrust, Ho - ly week who
Chorus.
See this com - bat all now must, Blow for blow, and
Allegro vivace.

quar - rel staid..... If for me your life were lost, Ev - er more would grief up -
quick - ly staid,.... Oh, that by a cut and thrust, Dun - ning cred - i - tors were
blade hath staid,.... On - ly with a sin - gle thrust, Your ac - count is quick - ly
dares in - vade? Be his quar - rel e'er so just, By the hal - ter 'twill be
blade to blade, Hap - py he who fall, who fall the

ff
- braid! If for me your life were lost, Ev - er more would grief up - braid!
paid, Oh, that by a cut and thrust, Dun - ning cred - i - tors were paid.
paid, On - ly with a sin - gle thrust, Your ac - count is quick - ly paid.
paid, Be his quar - rel e'er so just, By the hal - ter 'twill be paid.
first, Con - quest by the hang - man paid, the hang - man paid.

f

Oh! for - bear, in - deed you must, Be this fright - ful

Oh! you soon shall bite the dust, Hon - or's debt is

Come you will not prove the first, Brag - gart whom this

Don't for - get be - fore you thrust, Ho - ly week who

Sopranos.

Tenors.
See this com - bat all now must, Blow for blow and

quar - rel staid, If for me your life were lost,

quick - ly staid! Oh, that by a cut and thrust,

blade hath staid, On - ly with a sin - gle thrust,

dares in - vade! Be his quar - rel e'er so just,

Unis.
blade for blade! Hap - py he who falls the first,

8va......

1st time. 2d time.

E - er more would grief up - braid! - braid! E - ver

Dun - ning cred - i - tors were paid! paid! Oh! that

Your ac - count is quick - ly paid! paid! On - ly

By the hal - ter will be paid! paid! Be his

Sopranos.

Tenors.
Con - quest by the hang - man paid! paid! Hap - py

8va. . . . .

more would grief up - braid! E - er more would grief up -

by a cut and thrust, Dun - ning cred - i - tors were

with a sin - gle thrust, Your ac - count is quick - ly

quar - rel e'er so just, By the hal - ter will be

he who falls the first, Con - quest by the hang - man

8va. . . . .

- braid!   Ev - er   more   would   grief   up - braid...........

paid,   Dun - ning   cred - i - tors   were   paid...........

paid,   Your   ao - count   is   quick - ly   paid....... ....

paid,   By   the   hal - ter   'twill   be   paid...........

paid,   Con - quest   by   the   hang - man   paid.. ....

8va....................................loco.

(Exeunt L. 2. E., all but DON JOSE.)

stacc.   *f*

DON JOSE Have a care my worthy captain ; Don Cæsar is a dead thrust. I would not give a single maravedi for *your* share of daylight to-morrow.

[*Enter* MARITANA, R. U. E., *joyfully.*]

MAR. (*singing as she went out.*) You here, still, signor ? Ah, I have seen our beautiful Queen looking so amiable ! Diamonds, too, glittering brilliantly ! Delightful !

DON J. (*aside.*) This Gitana ! who knows ?—that fool, Don Cæsar too—they might be rendered subservient to my purpose ! (*To* MARITANA.) Still dreaming of greatness, eh ?

MAR. Ah, signor, if I had but your opportunity of going to court, and seeing all the splendor—why you might speak to the King !

DON J. I prefer speaking to you.

MAR. Me ! The time is badly chosen just now, for here are numbers of people who will require of me to tell their fortunes. Shall I tell yours, signor ?

DON J. By and by, (*apart*) anon you shall learn your own.

[*Enter People.*]

"PRETTY GITANA."

No. 8. CHORUS.

Pret-ty Gi-ta-na tell us, tell us, what the fates, the fates de-cree.

Pret-ty Gi-ta-na tell us, tell us, what the fates, the fates de-cree.

shall I mar-ried be?

Pret-ty Gi-ta-na tell us, tell us shall we, shall we, shall we hap-py be?

Pret-ty Gi-ta-na tell us, tell us shall we, shall we, shall we hap-py be?

shall I mar - ried be?

Pret - ty Gi - ta - na shall we hap - py be? Pret - ty Gi - ta - na shall I mar - ried be?

Pret - ty Gi - ta - na shall we hap - py be? Pret - ty Gi - ta - na shall I mar - ried be?

Pret - ty Gi - ta - na shall I wealthy be?

Pret - ty Gi - ta - na tell us, tell us, what the fates, the fates de - cree,

Pret - ty Gi - ta - na tell us, tell us, what the fates, the fates de - cree.

shall I mar - ried be?

Pret - ty Gi - ta - na tell us, tell us shall we, shall we, shall we hap - py be?

Pret - ty Gi - ta - na tell us, tell us shall we, shall we, shall we hap - py be?

MARITANA.

Yes, yes, the lan - guage of the skies, with ease can

I, can I im - part; But plain-er road, in star - ry eyes, The lau - guage of the heart.

With whom be - gins the charm? With

me! With me! with me! Young Sol - dier first your

With me! with me!

With me! with me! with me!

palm let me see!

You love a pret-ty dame, a pret-ty

Will-ing-ly, Will-ing-ly, that's

dame,   You   are   to   blame,   you   are   to   blame.

true.

p

a tempo.   *tr*   *tr*

.... Be - ware   of   woo - ing   an   old   man's wife,   an   old   man's

p

(*The* SOLDIER *turns away confused.*)

wife,   Her youth   and   beau - ty   will cause   you strife,   will cause   you

94

Chorus.

strife. Be-ware of woo - ing an old man's wife, an old man's wife, Her

Be-ware of woo - ing an old man's wife, an old man's wife, Her

youth and beau - ty, will cause you strife, will cause you strife.

youth and beau : ty, will cause you strife, will cause you strife.

Who next, who next pur - sues the charm! Tell me!

Tell me!

Tell me!

MARITANA. (to an old man.)

Tell me! Good Fa - ther now your palm, your palm, you have a

Tell me!

OLD MAN.

Tell me Cheer - ful-ly, cheer - ful-ly,

8va loco.

piu lento.

hand - some bride, Of beau - ty she's the pride, the

that's true, that's true!

pp

pride, When weak old do - tards to young maids wed, to young maid

wed. Young men do some - times make love in- stead, make love in -

OLD MAN. Bah! (*As he turns away the people laugh. Exit* OLD MAN.)

- stead. When weak old do - tards to young maids wed, to young maids wed, Young

When weak old do - tards to young maids wed, to young maids wed, Young men do some - times make love in - stead, make love , in - stead.

men do some - times make love in - stead, make love in - stead.

DON JOSE.

In turn what say you............ shall I tell............ your fortune?

MARITANA. (smiling.)

With all .... my heart,............ With all............. my heart.

DON JOSE.

At · tend....... .... I pray you!

DON JOSE.

It is in - deed your for - tune............ I now

im - - part.... .... To you I prom - ise rank,

I prom - - ise rank, A car - riage,

a splen - did E - quip - age................................

And speed-y marriage. Mar - - riage, O joy! all my

heart de-sires, O joy,........ all my heart de-sires ... Glad - ly I

hear.............. the stars'............ de - cree .... On - ly I fear this

gold - en hope,........ on - ly I fear this gold - en hope, Is far........ too bright.......... too bright.................. for me..........

A - maz'd.............. in - deed; I tell but what's.......... de -

creed, as you shall see. De-creed by whom?........ By me........ ...

DON JOSE.

MARITANA.

DON JOSE.

102

MARITANA.

by thee! by thee!   by thee! by thee!.........

DON JOSE.

.... by me!   Yes, yes!   by me!

tr (With delight.)

Ah! ah, more than that with-

Ah! ah, bet-ter than that with-

- in my hand, Ah, more than that with-in my hand, Al-most........ a

- in thy hand, bet-ter than that with-in thy hand, Al-most........ a sovre; ...... high ...... com·mand ...... A prince-ly heart, a

scep - tre; ...... high ...... com·mand ...... A prince-ly heart, a

Pal - ace home, A Prince-ly heart, a Pal-ace home, The mir - ror'd

Pal - ace home, A Prince-ly heart, a Pal-ace home, The mir - :or'd

ball, ... the glit - - t'ring dome, the ......

ball, the glit-t'ring dome, ... the glit-t'ring dome, the ......

glit - t'ring dome, the glit - t'ring dome,........

glit - t'ring dome, the glit - t'ring dome,........

The............ glit - - t'ring........ dome......—

The ... . glit - - t'ring........ dome————

"FAREWELL, MY GALLANT CAPTAIN."

No. 9.   FINALE TO ACT I.

(Enter Soldiers and People.)

Allegro molto.

(Enter Don Cæsar. L. 2. e.)   *Meno vivo.*

Fare-well,.... my gal-lant Cap-tain! I told you how 'twould be;

Fare-well, my val-lant Cap - tain! I told you how 'twould be;   Fare-

... well, my gallant Cap - tain! I told you how 'twould be; Farewell, my gallant Cap - tain! I told you how 'twould be; You'll not for - get the les - son due to me, you'll not for - get the les - son due to me, Fare-well my gal - - lant Cap - - tain! I told .... you, I told you how...... 'twould be.

MARITANA.

Midst of this

(*Enter* LAZARILLO, L. 2 E., *troubled.*)

Th'Al-ca-de and the sol - diers, You they seek, I fear. Th'Al

D. JOSE.

Yes, by the name, the name of the

tu - mult and strife, scarce half a - wake I seem: The words that you have said, still paint the gold - en

(*to* D. JOSE.)

- - ca-de and the sol - diers, you they seek I fear, Th'Al-ca-de and the sol - diers, you they seek, I

king swear I, the dream,.......... the gold-en dream, whene'er thou wak'st a -

MARITANA (L. C.)

dream the words that you have said, that you have said, the words that

LAZARILLO (R. C.)

fear, you they seek I fear............ Th' Al-ca - - de

D. CÆSAR (R.)

Then I an - oth - - er jour - ney must take!

D. JOSE (L.)

- - gain, shall on thee bright - ly beam,............ when-e'er thou

you have said, that you have said, still paint,............ still paint the

and the sol - - diers, you they seek

Then I an - oth - - er jour - ney must take, must take!

wak'st a - - gain,................ shall on thee bright - -

gold - - en dream,............... still paint the gold - - - - en dream.

I fear,................. you they seek............. I fear.

Then I an-oth - er jour - ney must take; that's pret - ty clear.

- - ly beam, shall on thee bright - - - - ly beam.

Enter ALCADE (L. U. E.)

Stay!

piu mosso.

In the name of the King I you.... arrest! Sir, stay, I you ar-rest! Sir,

114

MARITANA.
Mid'st of this tu - mult and strife, scarce half awake I seem a -

LAZARILLO.
Why in the name of the King a no - ble Lord thus stay, A

DON CÆSAR.
Well in the name, the name of the King since you arrest I stay, since

DON JOSE.
Yes by the name of the King, swear I the golden dream, the

ALCADE.
stay. Your sword at once re-sign, your sword at once re-sign, at

SOPRANOS.
Why in the name of the King a no - ble Lord thus stay, a

TENORS.
Why in the name of the King a no - ble Lord thus stay, a

BASSES.
Why in the name of the King a no - ble Lord thus stay, a

.. wake I seem, the words that you have said still paint the gold - en dream....

noble Lord, thus stay; why in the name, why in the name, why in the name

you ar-rest I stay; my sword I thus re - sign, and now the laws, and now the

gold - en dream, when - e'er thou wak'st a - gain, thou wak'st a - gain, shall on thee bright - ly

once re - sign, your sword at once re - sign, at once re - sign, and now the laws, the

noble Lord, thus stay; why in the name, why in the name, why in the name

noble Lord, thus stay; why in the name, why in the name, why in the name

noble Lord, thus stay; why in the name, why in the name, why in the name

8va

112

.... the golden dream, still paint the gold - en the gold - en dream, still paint the gold - en
Lord thus stay! I,.... Don Cæ-sar, Don Cæ-sar de - fend I,.... Don Cæ-sar, Don Cæ-
(to people.)
laws o-bey! de-sist I pray! de - sist I pray! yes, I o-bey, I o-
bright - ly beam, swear I the dream, the gold - en dream shall on thee
laws - o - bey, the laws o - bey, the laws o - bey, the laws o - bey, the
thus stay! we Don Cæ-sar, Don Cæ-sar de - fend, we.... Don Cæ-sar, Don Cæ-
thus stay! we Don Cæ-sar, Don Cæ-sar de - fend, we.... Don Cæ-sar, Don Cæ-
8va

114

gold-en dream.

a piacere.

Ah!...... what do my eyes be-

- - sar de-fend, If he the word, the word but say.

- - bey, yes I o-bey, yes I o-bey, yes I o-bey.

bright-ly beam.

laws o-bey, a-way, a-way, a-way, a-way.

- - sar de-fend, If he the word, the word but say.

- - sar de-fend, If he the word, the word but say.

- - sar de-fend, If he the word, the word but say.

hold,
Meno Allegro.
ff
p
MARITANA.
Free the gal - lant cap - tive, pray; Free the gal - lant cap - tive pray;
I, to-mor - row, shall have gold, Glad - ly I'll his ran - som pay, I, tomor - row,
shall have gold, Glad - ly I'll his ran - som pay, glad - ly I'll his ran - som pay.
cres.

LAZARILLO.

MARITANA.
Free the gal - lant cap - tive, pray ; Glad - ly I'll his ran - som pay. . .
CHORUS.
Oh ! mis - for - tune for this quar - rel
Oh ! mis - for - tune for this quar - rel
D. CÆSAR.
Gen' - rous creature they'll not hear you.
MARITANA.
I'll with gold his ran - som pay.
D. CÆSAR.
All good An - gels
Oh ! mis - for - tune ! for this quar - rel, must his
Oh ! mis - for - tune ! for this quar - rel, must his

MARITANA.

I, to-mor-row, shall have gold, Glad-ly I'll his ran-som pay.

hov-er near you all must die of some-thing some day 'Tis a debt we all must pay.

life, his life ig no - bly pay, ig - no - bly pay.

life, his life ig no - bly pay, ig - no - bly pay.

cres.

ALCADE.

March! by or - der of the King, I, you ar - rest Sir, stay, I, you ar - rest sir,

_f_

MARITANA.

I'll with gold his ransom pay, with gold his ransom pay, his ran - som pay, with gold his ransom pay, with

LAZARILLO.

Why in the name of the King, a no - ble Lord thus stay, a noble Lord thus stay, why in the name, why in the

D. CÆSAR.

Well in the name of the King since you arrest, I stay, since you arrest I stay, my sword I thus resign, and

D. JOSE.

Well in the name of the King since he ar - rest I pray your sword at once resign, your sword at once resign, and

ALCADE.

stay your sword at once resign, your sword at once resign, and now the laws obey, your sword at once, resign, and

Why in the name of the King, a no - ble Lord thus stay, a noble Lord thus stay, why in the name, why in the

Why in the name of the King, a no - ble Lord thus stay, a noble Lord thus stay, why in the name, why in the

Why in the name of the King, a no - ble Lord thus stay, a noble Lord thus stay, why in the name, why in the

gold his ran-som   pay, his ransom pay, with gold his ransom pay, with gold his ran-som   pay, his ransom pay, I'll   with

name, why in the name of   the King, a noble Lord, a no-ble Lord thus stay, a noble Lord thus stay, I   Don Cæ

now the laws, and   now the laws o-bey, my sword I now resign, and   now the laws, and now the laws obey, desist   I

now the laws o- bey, the laws   o bey, your sword at once resign, and and now the laws o - bey, the laws   o - bey, the laws o -

now the laws o- bey, the laws   o-bey, your sword at once resign, and now the laws o- bey, the laws   o. bey, a-way! a -

name, why in the name of   the King, a noble Lord, a no-ble Lord thus stay, a noble Lord thus stay, we   Don Cæ

name, why in the name of   the King, a noble Lord, a no-ble Lord thus stay, a noble Lord thus stay, we   Don Cæ

name, why in the name of   the King, a noble Lord, a no-ble Lord thus stay, a noble Lord thus stay, we   Don Cæ

gold his ran-som pay, I'll with gold his ran-som pay, his ransom pay, his ran-som pay.

- sar, Don Cæsar de - fend, I Don Cæsar, Don Cæsar defend, If he the word, the word but say.

pray the laws o - bey, no I I o - bey, the laws o-bey, the laws o - bey, the laws o - bey.

- bey, the laws o - bey, the laws o - bey, the laws o - bey, the laws o - bey, the laws o - bey.

-way! the laws o - bey, a - way! a - way! the laws o - bey, the laws o - bey, the laws o - bey, a - way!

- sar, Don Cæsar defend, we Don Cæsar, Don Cæsar defend, If he the word, the word but say.

- sar, Don Cæsar defend, we Don Cæsar, Don Cæsar defend, If he the word, the word but say.

- sar, Don Cæsar defend, we Don Cæsar, Don Cæsar defend, If he the word, the word but say.

tutta la forza.

Oh! mis-for-tune for this quar-rel, Oh! mis-for-tune for this quar-rel, Oh! mis-for tune

Oh! mis-for-tune for this quar-rel, Oh! mis-for-tune for this quar-rel, Oh! mis-for-tune

All must die of something some day, all must die of something some day, 'Tis a debt that

I forewarn'd him for the quarrel, I forewarn'd him for the quar-rel, he with life must

Cease this fol-ly, cease this fol-ly, cease this fol-ly, on a-way! he with life must

Oh! mis-for-tune for this quar-rel, Oh! mis-for-tune for this quar-rel, must his life ig-

Oh! mis-for-tune for this quar-rel, Oh! mis-for-tune for this quar-rel, must his life ig-

Oh! mis-for-tune for this quar-rel, Oh! mis-for-tune for this quar-rel, must his life ig-

for this quarrel must his life ig - no - bly pay ! Oh ! mis-for - tune for the quar - rel

for this quarrel must his life ig - no - bly pay ! Oh ! mis-for - tune for the quar - rel

all must pay, 'Tis a debt we all must pay, all must die of something some day,

sure - ly pay, he with life must sure - ly pay, I forewarn'd him, for the quar - rel

sure - ly pay, he with life must sure - ly pay, Cease this fol - ly on, a - way,

- no - bly pay, must his life ig - no - bly pay, Oh ! mis-for - tune for the quar - rel

- no - bly pay, must his life ig - no - bly pay, Oh ! mis-for - tune for the quar - rel

- no - bly pay, must his life ig - no - bly pay, Oh ! mis-for - tune for the quar - rel must his life ig - no - bly pay, must his life ig - no - bly pay, Ig -

must his life ig - no - bly pay, must his life ig - no - bly pay, Ig -

'Tis a debt that all must pay, 'Tis a debt that all must pay, that

must his life ig - no - bly pay, must his life ig - no - bly pay, must

he with life must sure - ly pay, he with life must sure - ly pay, must

must his life ig - no - bly pay, must his life ig - no - bly pay, Ig -

must his life ig - no - bly pay, must his life ig - no - bly pay, Ig -

must his life ig - no - bly pay, must his life ig - no - bly pay, Ig -

più mosso.
- no - - bly pay. Oh! mis - for - tune for this
- no - - bly pay. Oh! mis - for - tune for this
all must pay. All must die of some - thing
sure - - ly pay. I fore - warn'd him of this
sure - - ly pay. Cease this fol - ly, on, a-
- no - - bly pay. Oh! mis - for - tune for this
- no - - bly pay. Oh! mis - for - tune for this
- no - - bly pay. Oh! mis - for - tune for this
Marcato il Basso.

1st.
quar - rel, must his life, his life ig - no - bly pay.
quar - rel must his life, his life ig - no - bly pay.
some day, 'Tis a debt that all must pay.
quar - rel, he with life must sure - ly pay.
- way! a - way! he with life must sure - ly pay.
quar - rel must his life his life ig - no - bly pay.
quar - rel must his life, his life ig - no - bly pay.
quar - rel must his life, his life ig - no - bly pay.

2d.
pay, I'll with gold to - mor-row pay, to - mor - row pay, I'll with gold to - mor - row
pay, Oh! mis - for - tune must his life Ig - no - - bly pay. Oh, mis - for - tune must his
pay, Gen'rous crea - ture, they'll not hear you, All good
pay, I fore-warn'd him, for this quarrel he with life must sure - ly pay, I forewarn'd him for this
pay, Cease this fol - ly, cease this fol - ly or a - way, a - way, Cease this fol - ly, cease this
pay, Oh! mis - for-tune, must his life Ig - no - bly pay, Oh, mis - for-tune must his
pay, Oh! mis - for - tune must his life Ig - no - bly pay, Oh, mis - for - tune must his
pay, Oh! mis - for - tune must his life Ig - no - bly pay, Oh, mis - for - tune must his
8va loco.

128

pay, to - mor row pay, to - mor - row pay, To - mor - row

life ig - no - bly pay, Ig - no - bly pay, Ig - no - bly

an - gels hov - er round thee, a - way! I o - bey, a - way! I o -

quarrel he with life must sure - ly pay, must sure - ly pay, must sure - ly

fol - ly on a - way, a - way, a - way, a - way, a - way, a -

life Ig - no - bly pay, Ig - no - bly pay, Ig - no - bly

life Ig - no - bly pay, Ig - no - bly pay, Ig - no - bly

life Ig - no - bly pay, Ig no - bly pay, Ig - no - bly

(*Alcade and soldiers march, having* DON CÆSAR *in custody.*)

129

pay, To - mor - row pay, to - mor - row pay....................

pay, Ig - no - bly pay, Ig - no - bly pay...............

- bey, a - way! I o - bey a - way, a - way....................

pay, must sure - ly pay, must sure - ly pay...................

- way, a - way, a - way, a - way, a - way...................

pay, Ig - no - bly pay, Ig - no - bly pay.......... ....

pay, Ig - no - bly pay, Ig - no - bly pay...................

pay, Ig - no - bly pay, Ig - no - bly pay...................

Ped.

8va............... loco.

8va,

ACT. II.

ALAS! THOSE CHIMES SO SWEETLY STEALING.

No. 10.

Interior of a Fortress.—A window at back, opened, shows a clock (with the hour hand at five) on a neighboring tower.— DON CÆSAR *is discovered asleep on a couch,* (R.) LAZARILLO *near him.—Chimes heard.*

(*Before the Curtain rises.*)

ANDANTE.

p soave.

Symphony of the Song begins.

pp

Basso ben legato. 8ves.

8ves.

LAZARILLO.

A - las those chimes, so sweetly steal - ing, Gent -ly dul - cet,

gent - ly dul -cet, to the ear, Sound like pi -ty's voice re - veal - ing

To the dy -ing, death is near. Still he slumbers, how se - rene - ly!

Not a sigh disturbs his rest; Oh! that an -gels now might waft him

132

To the man-sions of the blest,   Oh! that an - gels now might waft him

To the mansions of the blest.   *ritard.*

ritard.

8ves.

Yes, yes those chimes   so soft - ly swell - ing,   As from some ho - ly

8ves.

sphere, as from some ho - ly sphere.   Sound like hymns of spir -its toll - ing

8ves.

To the dy-ing, peace is here. Come! a-bide with us in heav - en,

Here, no grief can reach thy breast, Come! ap-prov-ing an - gels wait thee,

In the man-sions of the blest, Come! ap-prov-ing an - gels wait thee,

In the mansions of the blest. *ritard.*

DON CÆSAR, (*waking.*) Ha! thou boy, tell me what o'clock is't.
[LAZ. *troubled, points to the clock.*]
DON CÆSAR. Still two hours to live. Deuce! what made me wake so early? Dreaming, too, my creditors were all transported to the moon. Ha! ha! Still two hours! Boy, how shall I pass the time?
LAZ. Signor?
DON CÆSAR. If but two hours of life were thy whole remain of grief or joy in this world—answer me truly, scapegrace—how would'st employ thyself—eh?
LAZ. (*bowing.*) Pardon, signor; I would send for a priest, and confess my sins.

DON CÆSAR. Ha! ha! What, confess my sins in two hours! Two hours might serve for thee, boy; but for me, two years would scarce suffice. Well thought—I'll make my will—no, that would scarce occupy two minutes.
LAZ. Alas! and is there no one, signor, might supplicate the King to spare thy life?
DON CÆSAR, (*reflecting*) No, no, boy! No one cares whether I'm shot or hanged!
LAZ. No one?
DON CÆSAR. No one! Yes—one—
LAZ. (*eagerly.*) Oh! name him.

"HITHER AS I CAME."

No. 11.

Moderato.

Hi-ther as I came, one poor old man

With sil - ver hairs, and tear-drops in his eyes, Wept that my life was

wast-ed to a span, And mer - cy, and mer-cy im-por-tun'd with bit-ter cries. Thy Fa-ther!

Fran - tic were his looks! That poor old man with sil - ver hairs, grief's ac - cents on his tongue; Lost in des - pair, grief's ac - cents on his tongue.

Lost in des - pair, be - fore the guard he ran. Lost in des - pair, be -

- fore the guard he ran, And held a doc-u - ment, at least, at least so long.

LAZARILLO. *a piacere.*

His sad pe - ti - tion, thee to guard from ill!

Don Cæsar. (Affects to weep.) a piacere. Allegretto.

It was, a - las! It was, a - las! an un - paid Tai - lor's bill. Ha!

ha! ha! ha! ha! ha! this one e - ter - nal dun Tor - ment of earth, I shall at least out

ruu....

"TURN ON, OLD TIME."

No. 12.   Don Cæsar.

Turn on, old Time,.... .... thine hour - glass,... the sand of
life,........... of life, why stay?........... Turn on, old Time,...................... thine
hour - glass,.... the sand of life, ... of life, why stay?.......... Quick! let the

gold......... ..... grain'd mo-ments pass,............ 'Tis they all debts,........... all debts must

pay,............ quick! let the gold............ grain'd mo ments pass,............ 'Tis they all

rall.   *tempo.*

debts,............ all debts must pay..........

Lazarillo.
Stay, fleet - ing time,............ .... thine hour - glass,.... the tide of life,..........
.... of life, oh stay!........... Nor let his gold - - - - - - en moments pass,..
.... like worthless sand,............. like sand a - way............. Stay, fleet - ing time, ...
8va.
.............thine hour - glass,..... The tide of life,............. of life, oh stay!........
8va.

140

Nor let the gold - - - - en mo-ments pass.......... like worthless sand,........

8va.

.... like sand a - way...........

(*Enter* Don Jose, c.)

LAZARILLO. (L.)

For him, oh be........ .... there ma - ny years,........... A - part, a - part...........

DON CÆSAR. (R.)

Of what a - vail............ are grief and tears,............ are grief and tears...........

DON JOSE. (C.)

Des-pite, old Time,........... thine hour - glass, turn

from ev'- ry woe,........... Nor let his gold - - en mo- ments pass........

since life must go?.... .... Quick! let the gold............ grain'd mo- ments pass .....

quick- ly as it may,............ His sand of life............. not yet shall pass.........

like worth-less sand,........... like sand a - way............ For him, oh!

'tis they all debts,......... all debts must pay............ Of what a - vail.............

If he my wish,.......... my wish o - bey........... Of life there

be there ma - ny years............ a - part, a - part............ from ev' - ry woe..........

.... are grief and tears....,......... since life, since life............. which came must go,..........

are full hap - py years............. if well the die,............. the die we throw.......

8va.

the blue se - rene which heav- en wears............. when waves scarce ebb,..........

.... and brief the long - - - - est tide of years............ as waves scarce ebb,..........

For May-day smiles and au - tumn tears............... are waves that ebb,..........

8va.

.... scarce ebb and flow,.... .... when waves scarce ebb and flow,..... ....

.... that ebb and flow, ... as waves that ebb and flow,.....................

.... that ebb and flow,.................. ..... are waves that ebb and flow,..................

.... when waves scarce ebb and flow,.......... scarce ebb and flow,......... scarce ebb and flow.

.... are waves that ebb and flow, ... flow.

.... are waves that ebb and flow,........... that ebb and flow,......... that ebb and flow.

(*At a gesture from* DON JOSE, LAZARILLO *exits,* L.)

DON CÆSAR. Don Jose in my prison !

DON JOSE. Ought that to surprise you ? Am I not an old friend ? As first minister, I would exert my influence to serve you.

D. CÆSAR. Serve me ! (*Looking at clock.*) I have scarcely two hours to live.

D. JOSE. Have you no last request ?

D. CÆSAR. Um ! none. (*Recollecting.*) Yes ; yonder boy, who has just quitted us, I, somehow, take au interest in his

D. JOSE. Is he not the cause of your death ?

D. CÆSAR. Inadvertently. I owe him that — but, then, I owe something to everybody.

D. JOSE. You wish me to take the lad into my service, perhaps ?

D. CÆSAR. That is my wish.

D. JOSE. It shall be done ; what more ?

D. CÆSAR. Nothing.

D. JOSE. No ! Is the last of the Garofas, then, content to perish like —

D. CÆSAR. (*troubled.*) Hush ! I fear to think of such ignominy. If his Majesty would but confer upon me the happiness of falling like a soldier.

YES! LET ME LIKE A SOLDIER FALL.

No. 13.   Don Cæsar.

Tempo di Marcia.

DON CÆSAR.

Yes ! let me like a Sol - dier fall, Up - on some o - pen plain, This breast ex - panding for the

ball, To blot out ev' - ry stain. Brave man - ly hearts con - fer my doom, That gent - ler ones may tell; How-e'er for - got, un - known my tomb, I, like a Sol - dier

fell, How - e'er for - got, un - known my tomb, I, like a Sol - dier

fell, I, like a Sol - - dier fell.

I ou-ly ask of that proud race, Which ends its blaze in me, To die the last, and not dis-

-grace its an--cient chi-val-ry! Tho' o'er my clay no ban-ner wave, Nor

trum-pet re-quiem swell, E-nough! they mur-mur o'er my grave, He, like a Sol-dier

fell, E---nough! they mur-mur o'er my grave, He, like a Sol-dier fell,   He, like a Sol - - dier fell.

Drums.

DON JOSE. I pledge my honor to see this performed, on condition—

DON CÆSAR. Condition to me! What is it?

D. JOSE. You must marry—

D. CÆSAR. Marry! I! What, for an hour and three-quarters? You are jesting.

D. JOSE. No! Quite the contrary.

D. CÆSAR. Ah! then, I see, it's my name you require?

D. JOSE. Perhaps—

D. CÆSAR. To elevate some antique maiden, who sighs to become a countess—fifty years of age, no doubt?

D. JOSE. It is immaterial to you.

D. CÆSAR. And ugly as a gorgon, eh?

D. JOSE. You will never behold her.

D. CÆSAR. How! Am I to marry an invisible woman?

D. JOSE. Her features will be rendered invisible to you by a thick veil, which will also prevent her seeing you; but you must give your honor not even to demand her name. Will you consent to take such a woman for your wedded wife?

D CÆSAR. I will! and I give my *word* to ask no questions whatever. Ha! ha! And why *not* marry? Mind, on condition that I am to be *shot* instead of *hanged.*

D. JOSE. Agreed.

D. CÆSAR. And that I see and carouse with the brave fellows commissioned to dispatch me!

D. JOSE. Strange request! however, be it so; a banquet shall be served, and your guards attend; and, as your costume is somewhat unbridegroomlike, you'll find apparel more suiting the occasion, in yonder chamber. (*Points* R. II. D.) Please you, put it on.

D. CÆSAR. Oh! by all means. Attention to costume is necessary when one becomes a bridegroom. Ha! ha!

[*Exit* R. II. D.

D. JOSE. Yes, yes, ma belle Maritana, my prediction of thy advancement cometh quickly to pass—married to Don Cæsar, the *widowed* Countess of Garofa may approach so near the King, as to be ever fascinating his eyes and heart—but will Maritana consent to this blindfold marriage? I'll tell her 'tis the Queen's *command.*

[*Enter* LAZARILLO, (L.) *giving a paper to* DON JOSE.]

D. JOSE. For me! (*Opens and reads it aside.*) Um! the King's pardon for Don Cæsar! It will not suit the first minister's policy that this should arrive at present. (*Puts it in his vest.*) Boy, at the request of Don Cæsar, I admit you at once into my service.

LAZ. Thanks, signor—*to-morrow.*

D. JOSE. Why not to-day?

LAZ. To-day, he lives, who dies, alas, for me! I cannot forsake him till—(*agitated.*) To-morrow, signor, I shall be as devoted to your service, as I am now to his.

D. JOSE. As thou pleasest. Go, tell them at the hotel, yonder, in my name, to serve a banquet for at least twenty, and say to the Captain of the Guard, I would speak to him in the outer room.

[*Exit* LAZARILLO (L.)

D. JOSE. It is a desperate game I am playing, but the very thought of possessing the Queen brings memory back to the happy time I first behold and loved her.

IN HAPPY MOMENTS DAY BY DAY.

No. 14.

D. JOSE.

In hap-py'moments day by day,   The
sands of life may pass,   In swift but tranquil tide a-way,   From time's un-er-ring glass.   Yet
hopes we used as bright to deem, Re-membrance will   re-call ;   Whose pure and whose unfading beam,   Is

dear - er than them all, Whose pure and whose un-fading beam, Is.... dear - er than them all.

rall.

Though anxious eyes up- on us gaze, And

f   p

hearts with foudness beat, Whose smile up- on each feature plays, With truth - ful-ness re - plete. Some

tho'ts none oth - er can replace, Re-membrance will re - call; Which in the flight of years we trace, Is dear - er than them all, Which in the flight of years we trace, Is .... dear - er than them all.

rall.

(Exit DON JOSE, DOOR IN FLAT.)

mf

(Enter LAZARILLO.*)*

LAZ. How strange ! a sumptuous banquet to be given ! this must be some mistake—some—

(Enter DON CÆSAR, *in a costly dress,* R H.D.)

LAZ. *(seeing* DON CÆSAR, *and staring.)* I'm not awake !

(Enter SERVANTS, *spreading a costly table,* R. *others with seats, then* SOLDIERS, &c. *The latter put aside their arquebusses behind the screen, then fill, drink, &c.)*

D. CÆSAR, *(gaily.)* Ah, boy ! why, how you stare ! Saw'st thou never a nobleman in velvet and gold before ? Ah ! here comes our guests and the banquet ! Bravo, Don Jose ! Welcome, friends ! welcome to table ! fill quickly !

LAZ. *(troubled.)* Alas ! whom see I ? Signor, 'tis the Alcade.

D. CÆSAR. He's welcome; bid him enter. (SOLDIERS *all rise.)*

(Enter ALCADE *and* OFFICERS, DOOR IN FLAT.)

ALCADE. Don Cæsar de Bazan ?

D. CÆSAR. I, sir, am he.

*(*ALCADE *gives sentence to* DON CÆSAR, *who reads it.)*

ALC. Your sentence now is changed. 'Tis the decree of the King, you be not hanged, but shot; there, 'neath the fortress wall. *(Pointing.)* You, sir, see it done, *(to* OFFICER,*)* at seven o'clock ; the warrant so commands.

(Exit, DOOR IN FLAT, OFFICERS *follow.)*

D. CÆSAR. So ; are they gone ? That affair's settled. Let us to our cups. *(Clock chimes six.)* Six, by the clock ! fill up and sing, no time to rehearse !

(Enter DON JOSE, DOOR IN FLAT, *conducting* MARITANA, *dressed as a bride, and veiled.)*

D. JOSE. Your bride !

D. CÆSAR, *(to* SOLDIERS, *laughing*) Fill ! long life and a happy widowhood to my future Countess!

LAZ. *(with surprise.)* His future Countess ?

D. CÆSAR. Aye, boy—why not ? A bumper to the Countess ! Fill *(Fills goblet.)*

"HEALTH TO THE LADY."

No. 15. QUARTET and CHORUS.

Allegro ma non troppo.

DON CAESAR.

Health to the La - dy, the love - ly bride, Length of years to her be giv - en!

CHORUS. TENORS & BASSES.

Health to the La - dy, the love - ly bride, Length of years to her be giv - en!

Like........ .... this bright - ly spark - ling nec - - tar,

Like........... this bright - ly spark - ling nec - - tar,

Ra - . diant with the light of hea - - ven,

Ra - . diant with the light of hea - - ven,

Don Cæsar.

Like........... this bright - ly spark - ling nec - tar,

Don Jose.

Life.... ..... on her each bliss be -

Ra - - - diant with the light of heav - en.

- stow. May........ her hours with joy o'er-

LAZARILLO. *ff*

Like this cup of ro - sy nec - tar, may her hours with joy o'er - flow.

- flow. Like this cup of ro - sy nec - tar, may her hours with joy o'er - flow.

Like this cup of ro - sy nec - tar, may her hours with joy o'er - flow.

ff

pp LAZARILLO.
Like . this cup .. .. of ro - - sy nec - tar,
pp DON CÆSAR.
Like .. .. .. this cup .... of ro - - sy nec - tar,
pp DON JOSE.
Like............ this cup............... of ro - - sy nec - tar,
pp CHORUS.
Like this cup of ro - sy nec - tar,
2d time tr
pp
May .... her hours........ with joy .... o'er - flow ... - flow....
2d time.
1st time.
May ...... her hours........ with joy............ o'er - flow.... - flow....
May........ her hours........ with joy............ o'er - flow.... - flow....
May her hours with joy o'er - flow, - flow.
1st. 2nd.
tr

ff
Health to the La - dy, the love - ly bride....
Health to the
ff
Health to the La - dy, the love - ly bride...
Health to the
ff
Health to the La - dy, the love - ly bride....
Health to the
ff
La - dy, the love - ly bride....
ppp
Health to the La - dy the
La - dy, the love - ly bride....
ppp
Health to the La - dy the
La - dy, the love - ly bride ...
ppp
Health to the La - dy the
pp

156

love - ly bride ... Health to the La - dy, the love - ly

love - ly bride.... Health to the La - dy, the love - ly

love - ly bride.... Health to the La - dy, the love - ly

bride.... ...

bride........

bride........

pp

(During this solo, LAZARILLO withdraws the bullets from the arquebusses.)

D. CAESAR

By this hand, this hand so soft and tremb- 'ling, By those

locks so sun - ny bright, 'Neath that veil, that

cru- el veil dis- sem- bling, Youth and beau - ty hide their

light, Youth and beau - ty hide their light.

MARITANA.

Like.... .... the mist, ... the mist up - on the moun - tain, so this

vell.... .... ob - scures........ my sight........ From............ this bo - - som

pal - - pi - ta - ting, Clos - ing ev - - 'ry beam of

light, Clos - ing ev - - 'ry beam of light.

p

MARITANA.
pp
Lo! the or - - - gan
LAZARILLO.
pp
Yes! the or - - - gan
DON CÆSAR.
pp
Lo! the or - - - gan
DON JOSE.
pp
Hark! the or - - - gan
CHORUS.
pp
Hark! the or - - - gan
Meno mosso.
p
hope in - spir - ing,
hope in - spir - ing,
sweet - ly peal - ing,
soft - ly peal - ing,
soft - ly peal - ing,

Call - eth to .. the hal - low'd rite .

Ah! .... what mys - ter -y, what

Call - eth to .... the nup - tial rite ..

Like .. ... a spir - it, a

Call - eth to ... the hal - low'd rite ..

Ah ! .... what mys - ter -y, what

Call - eth to ... the hal - low'd rite ....

Time .... is fly - ing,

Call - eth to .... the hal - low'd rite ...

Ah! what hear we,

a tempo.

cres.

ff

mys - te - ry, no es - cap - ing, I must be .... a bride .... to - night ....

spir - it seems to mur - mur, No, he shall .... not die ..... to - night ...

mys - te - ry, no es - cap - ing, I must wed, ... and die .... to - night ....

quick be stir - ring, You must wed, ... and die .... to - night ....

task re - volt - ing, He, by us, must fall to - night.

8va. .... *loco.*

Ah!........ what mys - ter-y, what mys-ter - y, no es - cap - ing, I must be .... a
Like....... a spir - it, a spir - it seems to mur - mur, No, he shall........ not
Ah!........ what mys - ter-y, what mys-ter - y, no es - cap - ing, I must wed,........ and
Time....... is fly - ing, quick be stir - ring, You must wed,.... and
Ah! what hear we, task re - volt - ing, He, by us, must
8va
bride to - night,.... I must be .... a bride to - night....
die to - night,.... No! he shall...... not die to - night,.... No!.... he shall not
die to - night,.... I must wed .... and die to - night, ... I .. must wed and
die to - night,.... You must wed ... and die to - night, You.... must wed and
fall to - night, He, by us, must fall to - night, . Ah! ... what hear we?
8va
loco.

die to - night..... No!... he shall not die to - night.....
die to - night..... I.... must wed and die to - night.....
die to - night..... You.... must wed and die to - night.....
task re - - volting! He,.... by us, must fall to - night.....
No!.... he shall not die to - night,...... No!.... he
Ah!.... what hear we? task re - - volting, He,.... by
pp

(*Clock chimes quarter past six, as all exeunt,* SOLDIERS *taking their arquebusses.*)

OH! WHAT PLEASURE.

No. 16. CHORUS.

SCENE II.—*A magnificent Saloon, in the Palace of the* MARQUIS MONTEFIORI, *brilliantly illuminated.* (C. D.) (R. H D.) (*Desk* L.)

Allegretto. Tempo di Polacca.

SOPRANOS.

Oh ! what pleasure, the soft gui - tar !

TENORS.

Oh ! what pleasure, the soft gui - tar !

BASSES.

Oh ! what pleasure, the soft gui - tar !

Oh! what pleas - ure, the soft, the soft gui -

Oh! what pleas - ure, the soft, the soft gui -

Oh! what pleas - ure, the soft, the soft gui -

- tar, And mer - ry cas - ta - net, and merry cas - - - ta -

- tar, And mer - ry cas - ta - net, and merry cas - - - ta -

- tar, And mer - ry cas - ta - net, and merry cas - - - ta -

p
pp
-net, Be - guile,.... be - guile the hours, while balm - y flow - ers, while balm - y
p
pp
-net, Be - guile, be - guile the hours, while balm - y flow - ers, while balm - y
p
pp
-net, Be - guile, be - guile the hours, while balm - y flow - ers, while balm - y
p
flowers And spark - - ling wine, with eyes that shine, that shine. Be-
p
flowers And spark - - ling wine, with eyes that shine, that shine. Be-
p
flowers And spark - - ling wine, with eyes that shine, that shine. Be-
p

-guile,.... be-guile the hours, while balm-y flow-ers, while balm-y flow-ers and

-guile, be-guile the hours, while balm-y flow-ers, while balm-y flow-ers and

-guile, be-guile the hours, while balm-y flow-ers, while balm-y flow-ers and

spark - - ling wine, with eyes that shine, with eyes that shine Like

spark - - ling wine, with eyes that shine, with eyes that shine Like

spark - - ling wine, with eyes that shine, with eyes that shine Like wand'ring stars to - geth - er met, Chase from the heart, Chase from the heart, all

wand'ring stars to - geth - er met, Chase from the heart, Chase from the heart, all

wand'ring stars to - geth - er met, Chase from the heart, Chase from the heart, all

sad re gret, all sad re - gret. Let true de - light, each bo-som cheer, Since not a care.... can here.

sad re-gret, all sad re - gret. Let true de - light, each bo-som cheer, Since not a care.... can here.

sad re-gret, all sad re - gret. Let true de - light, each bo-som cheer, Since not a care.... can here.

en - - ter here, can en - - ter here, can en - ter here, can en - ter
en - - ter here, can en - - ter here, can en - ter here, can en - ter
en - - ter here, can en - - ter here, can en - ter here, can en - ter
here, can en - ter here, can en - ter here.........................
here, can en - ter here, can en - ter here.........................
here, can en - ter here, can en - ter here.........................
8va

170

No. 17.

WALTZ.

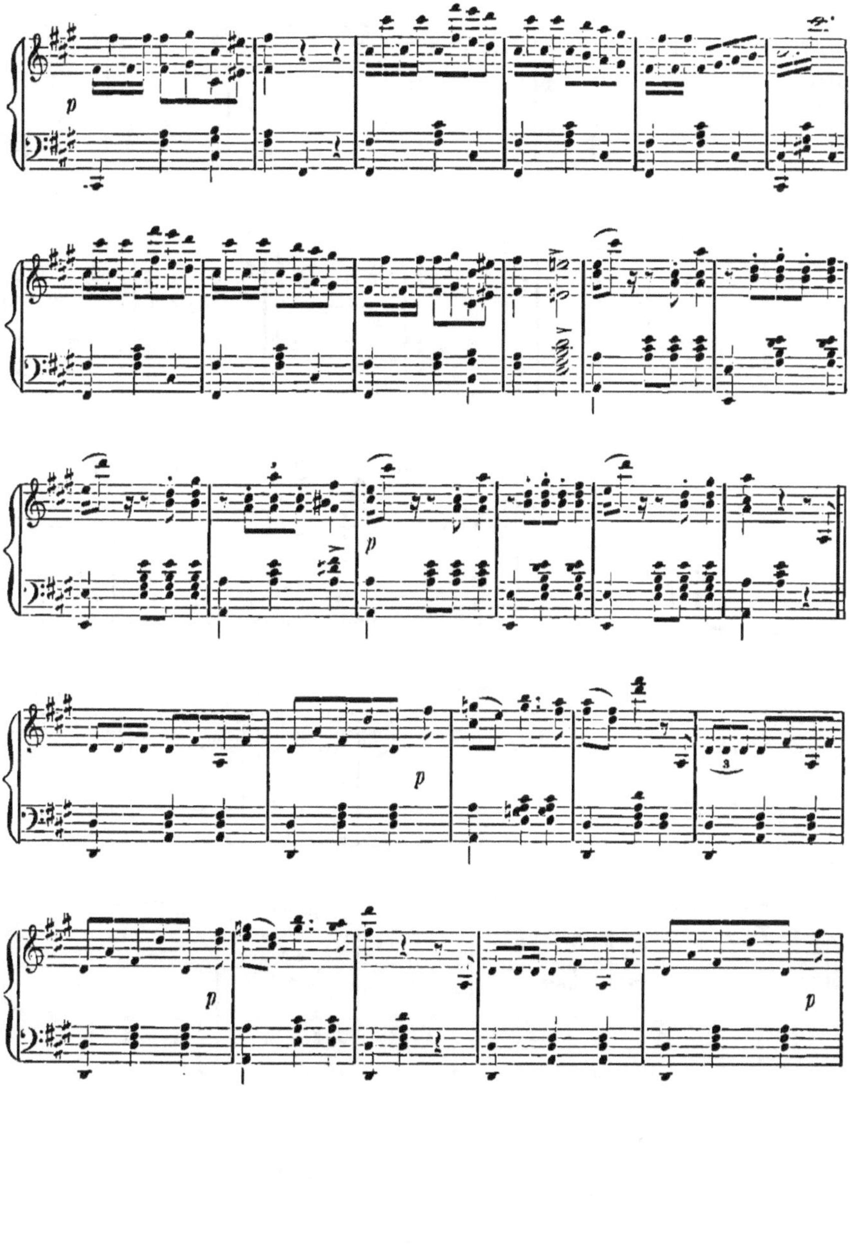
p
p
p
p
p

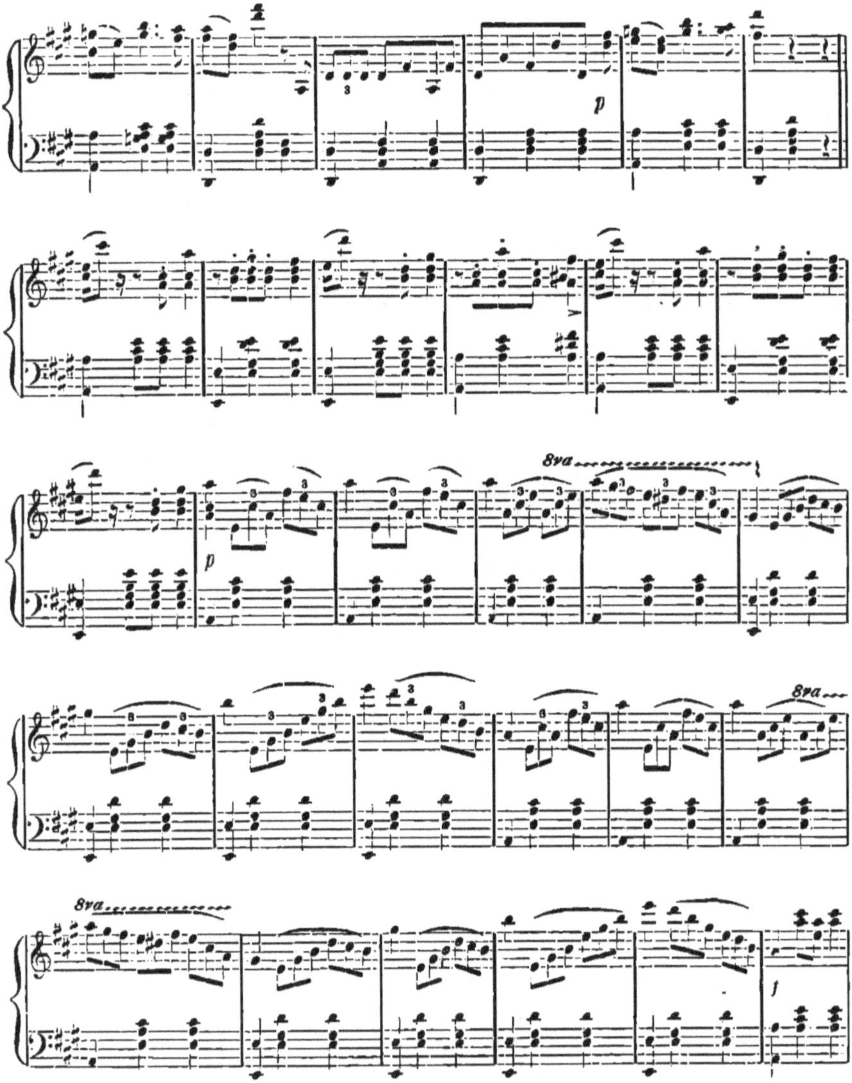
p
p
8va
8va
8va
f

During the waltz the fortress clock strikes seven; a roll of musketry is heard in the distance, the dance stops suddenly; MARCHIONESS advances.

MARCH. Holy Madelina, what sound was that? my nerves are absolutely aspen leaves.

MARQ. Sweet, my Lady Marchioness, subdue this terrific sensibility; yonder sound, fair excellence, was a — a mere nothing; some ruffianly soldier, for drawing his sword in Holy week, condemned (as one of my rascals informed me) to be shot at seven o'clock.

MARCH. (*with affectation.*) Dear me, Marquis, was that all. What a noise they make about trifles. Pray continue the dance.

MARQ. (*admiringly.*) Amiable creature.   [*Waltz resumed.*
                  (*Enter DON JOSE, C.D.R.*)

D. JOSE. Marquis!

MARQ. I'm enchanted to behold—

D. JOSE. Suppress these raptures, Monsieur le Marquis, and listen to me: I have conducted hither your *niece*, whom you lost some ten years ago.

MARQ. My niece? Impossible! I have no niece, signor.

D. JOSE. Oh yes, you have; when I gave you the appointment of Grand Director of the Royal Menagerie, you promised to recollect whatever I wished — stretch your memory a little, Monsieur le Marquis — I say you *have* a long lost niece.

MARQ. Oh, certainly, Don Jose; now you remind me, I recollect my pretty little niece well enough. Where is the dear infant?

D. JOSE. Infant? um! during ten years absence she is wonderfully grown up, of course.

MARQ. Certainly, she must be in such a lapse of time; where is she? I'm all impatience. Is she handsome? like the family?—does she resemble me?

D. JOSE. (*leading in MARITANA, C.D.L.*) Judge for yourself; here she is! Madame la Countess de Bazan. Madame— Monsieur le Marquis de Montefiori, your noble uncle.

MAR. A Marquis my—

MAR But I thought Don Cæsar de Bazan, at seven o'clock this evening, was expected to—

D. JOSE. Join the present party of course; yes, and this way, I perceive, he approacheth. You will apprise the Marchioness, your wife of the return of her lovely relative—I'll follow instantly, and—(*bows the MARQUIS out.*)

                  (*Enter the KING, R.U.D.*)

MAR. (*joyfully, then with chagrin.*) He! No! another?

D. JOSE. (*presenting MARITANA to the KING.*) The Countess! (*Bows, and goes up to the MARQUIS, who is explaining to the MARCHIONESS the suggestions of DON JOSE. The company is invited to withdraw, as if to take refreshments.*)

                  (*MUSIC, as all exit, C.D. but KING and MARITANA.*)

KING. Charming Maritana, my beauteous bride!

MAR. Bride!

KING. (*with great tenderness.*) Oh! yes: mine. I could not live without thee. It seemeth to me, beautiful Maritana, as if love's bright genius had but created thy sweet presence to render this world and earthly paradise.

"HEAR ME, GENTLE MARITANA."

No. 18.   The King.

Andante.   Vln. Solo.

THE KING.

Hear me, gentle Ma-ri - ta - na, By the magic of thy beau - ty Hear me swear, too fair Gi-

- ta - na, This fond heart beats but for thee.

Cap - tive 'neath thy chains de - light - ed.

dark and hea - vy,

Tho' its doom be dark and hea - vy By a smile of thine de-light - ed,

Would not if it could be free. By a smile of thine de-light - ed, Would not if it could be

Quasi Allegretto.

free..............

The Mar - i - ner ....
8va
loco.
tr
p
In his barque, When o'er him dim clouds hov - er, With rap - ture thro' tempest dark Be-
- holds one star a - bove, Sweet hope.... .. then his bosom swells, His ev'-ry care seems
a tempo.
o - ver, Sweet hope...... then his bosom swells, His ev'-ry care seems o - ver. A

smile, as from heaven, tells Of home, de-light and love. A smile, as from

heaven, tells Of home, delight and love. Sweet hope then his

bo - som swells, His ev' - - - ry

care seems o - ver, A smile, as from hea - ven, from

hea - - ven tells, Of home, of home, de -

- light and love.............. The Mar - i - ner........

8va ------ *loco.*

ad lib.

in his barque, When o'er him dim clouds hov - er, With rap - ture thro' tempest dark Be-

- holds oue star a - bove, Sweet hope.... .. then his bosom swells, His ev'-ry care seems

a tempo.

o - ver. Sweet hope...... then his bosom swells, His ev'- ry care seems o - ver. A

smile, as from heaven, tells Of home, de-light and love. A smile, as from

heaven, tells Of home, delight and love. A smile, as from heaven tells Of

home, delight and love. A smile, as from heaven, tells Of home, delight and love. A smile,   as from heaven, tells   Of home,   de - light and love.   A

smile,   as from heaven,   tells .... Of .... home,   delight and   love........ Of ....

home,   de - light and   love........   Of home,   de - light

cres.

and   love.................. .....

(*Enter* D. JOSE, *hastily*, C.D.L.)

D. JOSE, (*whispering*,) Sire, the guests return to the Saloon—withdraw, I beseech, or recognized—

KING. And Maritana?

D. JOSE, (*whispers*.) Her, at the appointed hour, you'll find at the Villa d'Aranguez—Sire, they come!

KING. I depart, remember! (*Gazing at* MARITANA.) Maritana! (*Sighs*.) [*Exit*, R.H.D.

MARI. (*joyfully*.) Gone! Am I free?

D. JOSE. Yes, he is gone! you are free (*aside*) till midnight. Go, join the festivity, and anticipate every happiness: they come to invite you.

(*Enter the* MARQUIS, L., *inviting* MARITANA *to join the dance*.)

MARQ. Sweet niece, shall we electrify them with a saraband, eh!

MARI. Dance? Willingly! The departure of yon dark stranger has removed a cloud from my heart; and a secret monitor whispers me, that a much dearer object is not far distant, whose presence will quickly confirm every anticipated joy. (*Exit* MARITANA *and* MARQUIS, C.D.L.)

D. JOSE. She little dreams that other is no more! (*exultingly*.)

(*Enter* DON CÆSAR, *disguised as a Monk*, C.D.)

D. CÆSAR, (*touching him*.) Don Jose!

D. JOSE. That voice! Who art thou?

D. CÆSAR, (*unmasking*.) Don Cæsar, at your service!

D. JOSE. Alive!

D. CÆSAR. Yes, some benevolent fairy, I presume, withdrew the bullets from the arquebusses; not liking to disgrace, I won't say disappoint, my executiouers, I fell; pretended to be shot, they walked away—I walked hither.

D. JOSE. For what purpose?

D. CÆSAR. To claim my wife.

D. JOSE. Your wife! who told you she was here?

D. CÆSAR, (*laughing*.) The same good fairy that withdrew the bullets from the arquebusses; where is she?

D. JOSE, (*pointing*, R.) In that room; find her out yourself.

D. CÆSAR. I will! Oh! I should know her from a thousand, if only by the softness of her small white hand.

(*Exit*, R.)

D. JOSE. How to mislead him?

(*Enter* MARQUIS, C.D.L.)

D. JOSE, (*aside*.) Ah! this creature!—(*Aloud*)—Where's your wife?

MARQ. Receiving the adulations of her adoring guests, as her lovely white hand touches the trembling lute! O—h!

(*Sighs*.)

D. JOSE. Ah! I have an appointment in my gift—Grand Master of the Aviary. Instruct the Marchioness to play a part as I direct, and the appointment is yours.

MARQ. I! Grand Master of the Royal Aviary, with a pension of—— What part is the divine Marchioness to play, Don Jose? Is it on the lute! She'll suspend your every faculty with a single chord!

D. JOSE. Bah! lute! no, no, I'll tell you. (*Exeunt*, L.)

(*Re-enter* DON CÆSAR, B)

D. CÆSAR.* I seek my wife in vain, for like some phantom she still eludes me. Thus are fondest hopes ever fading. Nought remains for me but dreamy memories,

* If following song is sung in the last act, substitute in place of above lines.

D. CÆSAR, (*angrily*.) No wife there. Don Jose is trifling with me. I'll demand satisfaction.

THERE IS A FLOWER THAT BLOOMETH.

No. 19. SONG.   Don Cæsar.

(NOTE.—This song was originally sung in the last Act. See * page 252.)

Andante.

There

is   a flow'r that   bloom - eth, When autumn leaves are shed;   With   the si - lent moon it

weep - eth, The spring   and sum - mer fled.   The ear - ly frost of   win - - ter,

Scarce its brow hath o - ver - cast; Oh! pluck it ere it wither, 'Tis the mem'ry of........ the

past, Oh! pluck it ere it wither,.... 'Tis the mem'ry, the mem'ry of the past.

It

waft - eth per - fume o'er us, Which few can e'er for - get; Of the bright scenes gone be-

188

-tore us, Of sweet, tho' sad re-gret! Let no heart brave its pow - - er, By

guil - ty thoughts o'er - cast, For then a poison'd flower, Is the mem'ry of........ the

past! For then a pois - on'd flower,.... Is the mem'ry, the mem'ry of the past.

(*Re-enter* Don Jose, L, *conducting in the* Marchioness *veiled, and followed by the* Marquis.)

D. Jose. The Countess de Bazan !

D. Cæsar. Ecstacy ! (*Aside.*) 'Tis her hand !

Marq. Eh? My wife Countess de Bazan ! And that the man whom they shot this very evening? I'm petrified ! I'll alarm all the —

D. Jose. Silence ! Remember the appointment.

"AH! CONFUSION."

No. 20. QUARTET.

(D. Cæsar *removes the veil.*)

D. Cæsar, (*with chagrin.*)

Ah ! con - fu - sion ! what de - lu - sion.

a tempo.

Ah ! con - fu - sion ! what de - lu - sion, with sur - prise I'm al - most mute,

Who would win her, let him wear her, I the prize will ne'er dis - pute.

D. Jose.

I the prize will ne'er...... dis - pute, This de - lu - sion, And con - fu - sion,

186

And re-gret will me just suit. He'll o-bey now, and not stay Now,

Ma - ri-ta-na to dis-pute. Ma - ri-ta-na to dis-pute.

MARCHIONESS.

Oh! vex-a - - tion, mor - - - ti-fi-ca - tion,

D. CÆSAR.

Ah! con - fu - - sion, what de - lu - sion,

D. JOSE.

This de - lu - - sion, and con - fu - sion,

MARQUIS.

Ah! con - fu - - sion, hence de - lu - sion,

With dis - dain I'm al - - - most mute.

With sur - prise I'm al - - - most mute.

And re - gret will me just suit.

Soon this sword shall all dis - pute.

Thus to scorn me can it borne be?

Who would win her, let him wear her,

He'll o - bey, now, and not stay now,

Thus to scorn thee, can it borne be?

Mar - quis, Mar - quis, He's a brute.

I the prize will ne'er dis - pute.

Ma - ri - ta - - na, to dis - pute.

Yes! dear crea - - ture, he's a brute.

Mar - quis, Mar - - quis, he's a brute!

I the prize will ne'er............. dis - pute!

Ma - ri - ta - - na to dis - pute!

Yes, dear crea - - ture, he's a brute.

cres

Oh vex - a - tion! Oh vex - a - tion! With dis-
Ah con - fu - sion! what de - lu - sion! With sur-
This de - lu - sion, and con - fu - sion, And re-
Ah con - fu - sion! hence de - lu - sion! Soon this
cen
- dain, I'm al - most mute! Oh vex - a - tion! Oh vex - a - tion! Oh vex-
- prise I'm al - most mute! Ah con - fu - sion! what de - lu - sion! Ah con-
- gret, will me just suit! This de - lu - sion, and con - fu - sion, this de-
sword, shall all dis - pute! Oh con - fu - sion! hence de - lu - sion! Oh de-
- do.
ff

- a - tion! with dis - dain I'm al - most mute, I'm al - most mute.

- fu - sion, with sur - prise I'm al - most mute, I'm al - most mute.

- lu - sion, this de - lu - sion me just suit, will me just suit.

- lu - sion! soon this sword, shall all dis - pute, shall all dis - pute.

cres.

Oh vex - a - tion! Oh vex - a - tion! With dis-

Ah con - fu - sion! what de - lu - sion! With sur-

This de - lu - sion, and con - fu - sion, And re-

Ah con - fu - sion! hence de - lu - sion! Soon this

cen

-dain, I'm al - most mute! Oh vex - a - tion! Oh vex - a - tion! Oh vex-
-prise I'm al - most mute! Ah con - fu - sion! what de - lu - sion! Ah con-
-gret, will me just suit! This de - lu - sion, and con - fu - sion, this de-
sword, shall all dis - pute! Oh con - fu - sion! hence de - lu - sion! Oh de-
ff
- a - tion! with dis - dain I'm al - most mute, I'm al - most mute.
- fu - sion, with sur - prise I'm al - most mute, I'm al - most mute.
- lu - sion, and re - gret will me just suit, will me just suit.
- lu - sion! soon this sword, shall all dis - pute, shall all dis - pute.

MARQ, (*touching his sword*.) I can scarcely restrain my rage.

D. CÆSAR, (*laughing*.) Don't be indignant on my account, good marquis. (*Whispering*.) But even you, who are twice my age, would prefer single-blessedness to a precious piece of antiquity for a wife like that.

MARQ. Antiquity! If you don't admire her yourself, don't attempt to dishearten others. (*Retreats angrily with* MARCHIONESS, C.D.)

D. JOSE. Then you renounce a bride who has married you for your name alone?

D. CÆSAR. Can you ask it?

D. JOSE. Don't be too hasty, be advised by a friend; your wife is rich; sign a contract to relinquish her, and quit Madrid for ever, and I'll ensure you an annual remittance of five thousand piastres.

D. CÆSAR. Pen, ink, and paper! 'tis done.

D. JOSE. They are here, write. (*Showing pens and ink on table.*) (DON CÆSAR *sits down at table,* L.)

D. CÆSAR, (*sitting*.) You have only to dictate.

D. JOSE, (DON CÆSAR, *repeating*.) Write I, Don Cæsar, Count de Garofa, consent to quit the Countess, my wife, (MARITANA *sings*) and Madrid, for ever, on payment of

(MARITANA *sings in the saloon,* DON CÆSAR *pauses to listen.*)

DON CÆSAR. Eh! what's that?

D. JOSE. Write! write!

THAT VOICE, 'TIS HER'S.

No. 21. FINALE TO ACT II.

Don Cæsar and Don Jose.

That voice, that voice, 'tis her's, 'tis her's I

Cæ - - sar, Cæ - sar, be - ware! Cæ - sar, be-

ff

swear, 'Tis her's, 'tis her's I swear, With whom I at the al - tar

- ware! be - ware! Cæ - sar, be - ware! Ere all thy danger may be

knelt, With whom I at the al - tar knelt. I'll seek my wife, I'll

felt, Ere all thy danger yet be felt. 'Twill cost thy life, 'Twill

(Drawing sword.)

seek, I'll seek my wife, I'll seek my wife.

cost, 'Twill cost thy life, 'Twill cost thy life.

cres.

ff

(*At a sign from* Don Jose, *a body of* Soldiers *enter* [c. d.] *and arrest* Don Cæsar.)

Don Jose. (*Pointing*)

Lo, a

p

crim - i - nal be - - fore you, Fled from

jus - tice, guard with life, guard with life.

DON CÆSAR.

But an in - - stant, I im - plore you, but an

in - - stant, I im - plore you, just to know, just to

know who is my wife! but an in - - stant I im -

DON JOSE.

No, no, no, it must not

ff

- plore you, but an in - - stant, I im - plore you, but an in - - stant, an
be, no, no, it must not be, no, no, it must not be, no,
in - - staut, just to know who is my wife?
no, it must not be, no, no, it must not be.
But an in - stant, but an in - stant, I im-
No, no, no, no, no, no, it must not

(*Enter* MARITANA, MARQUIS, MARCHIONESS *and guests.*)

-plore you, but no in - stant, I im -

be, no, no, it must not be, a - way! a - way! no, no, it must not be, a - way! a-

ff   *ff*

(*Enter* ALGUAZILS, *who detain* MARITANA *at the back.*)

-plore you, Her, let me see, her, let me see!

- way! her, ar - rest, too, Al - - gua- zils, there, Him to

stay, stay, stay, stay, stay......

meno mosso.

pris - on, Her, that way bear, to the Vil - la d'A-uan-Juez, a - way!......

pesante.

(Don Jose, Marquis *and* Marchioness *stand between* Maritana *and* Don Cæsar, *to prevent their seeing each other.*)

Adagio ma non troppo.

200

doth thus con-trol, what hor - ror now a - waits my soul? what myster-

doth thus con-trol, what hor - ror now a - waits my soul?

-trol................ this meet-ing would............... dis-tract my soul,

doth thus con-trol, not dark - er clouds, when thun - ders roll,

doth thus con-trol, not dark - er clouds, when thun - ders roll,

-y................ why thus con - trol, why thus con - trol,............ what hor - ror

what mys - ter - y must now con-trol, It tor - tures it dis -

what mys - ter - y Their steps con-trol, This meet - ing

what mys - ter - y doth thus con-trol, not dark - er clouds,

what mys - ter - y doth thus con-trol, not dark - er clouds,

202

soul .... what hor - ror now . . . . awaits my soul, . . . what mys - ter -
soul .... It tor - tures, it . . . . . . disturbs my soul, . . . what mys - ter -
soul................ this meet-ing would............... distract my soul, ... what mys - ter -
when thunders roll, not dark - er clouds when thunders roll, . . . what mys - ter -
when thunders roll, not dark - er clouds when thunders roll, . . . what mys - ter -
ff
- y.... why thus.... con - trol ... what hor - ror, what hor - ror now ... a - waits my
- y.... must now ... con - trol ... It tortures, it tor - tures, It ..... dis - tracts my
- y.... their steps.... con - trol.... this meeting, this meet - ing should.... dis - tract my
- y .. doth thus.... con - trol.... not dark er, not dark - er clouds .. when thun - ders
- y.... doth thus ... con - trol.... not dark er, not dark - er clouds when thun - ders
ff
p

pp
soul, what hor - ror now a - waits my soul, what hor - ror
soul, It tor - tures, it dis - tracts my soul, It tor - tures,
soul, this meet - ing would dis - tract my soul, this meet - ing
roll.
roll.
p
now a - waits my soul
it dis - tracts my soul
would, dis - tract my soul
ppp
not dark - er clouds, when thun - ders roll.
not dark - er clouds, when thun - ders roll.
dim.

Allegro vivace.
MARITANA. (Struggling.)
Who is he?................
Ah! let me
DON CÆSAR. (Struggling.)
Her, let me see,................
Ah! let me
DON JOSE.
A - way! ....
ff
8va
see,....................
Ah! let me see, ah!
see,. ....
Ah! set me free, ah!
A - way!........ a - way! no! no! it must not be, a - -
8va
p

let me see, I will be free, I will be free, I will be free, Ah!

set me free, Her, let me see, Her, let me see, I will be free, I

-way! It must not be, It must not be, no! no! it must not be, a-

let me see, I will, I will be free.....................................

will be free, I will, I will be free...............................

-way! it must not be, it must not be, a - - way! a - - - way!

pp **Bass Chorus.**

What ter - rors dread each heart con - trol, What con - ster - na - tion fills each

p **Tenors.**

What ter - rors

soul, What ter - rors dread each heart con - trol, What con - ster - na - tion fills each soul, What ter - rors

dread each heart con - trol, What con - ster - na - tion fills each soul, What ter - rors dread each heart con -

dread each heart con - trol, What con - ster - na - tion fills each soul, What ter - rors dread each heart con -

208

MARITANA.

Ah! what ter - rors dread each heart con - trol, what con - ster -

DON CÆSAR.

Ah! what ter - rors dread each heart con - trol, what con - ster -

- way! her ar - rest quick, All gua - zils there, her ar -

soul, what ter - rors dread each heart con trol, what con - ster -

soul, what ter - rors dread each heart con - trol, what con - ster -

- na - tion fills each soul, Ah! let me see, ah! let me

- na - tion fills each soul, Her let me see, her let me

- rest, quick, quick a - way! Quick quick a - way, Quick, quick a -

- na - tion fills each soul, what ter - rors dread each heart con -

- na - tion fills each soul, what ter - rors dread each heart con -

ff

see, Ah! let me free, I will be free............... I

see, Ah! let me free, I will be free I

- way! no, no, no, no, It must not be.................. no,

- trol, what con - ster - na - tion fills each soul, ... what con - ster -

- trol, what con - ster - na - tion fills each soul, ... what con - ster -

Più presto.

will, I will be free, Ah! what ter - rors dread con -

will, I will be free, Ah! what ter - rors dread con -

no, It must not be, Him a - way to Pris - on

- na - tion, fills each soul, Ah! what ter - rors dread con -

- na - tion, fills each soul, Ah! what ter - rors dread con -

- trol, Ah! what ter - rors dread con - trol, what con - ster - na - tion
- trol, Ah! what ter - rors dread con - trol, what con - ster - na - tion
bear, him a - way to Pri - son bear, a - way to Pris - on
- trol, Ah! what ter - rors dread con - trol, what con - ster - na - tion
- trol, Ah! what ter - rors dread con - trol, what con - ster - na tion
fills each soul, what con - ster - na - tion fills each soul, what con - ster -
fills each soul, what con - ster - na - tion fills each soul, what con - ster -
bear, a - way to Pri - son bear, a - way to Pri - son bear, a -
fills each soul, what con - ster - na - tion fills each soul, what cou - ster -
fills each soul, what con - ster - na - tion fills each soul, what con - ster -
ff
ped.

1st.
-na - - - tion fills each soul,
-na - - - tion fills each soul,
-way to pri - son bear, a - way,
-na - - - tion fills each soul,
-na - - - tion fills each soul,
1st.
2d.
soul, what ter - rors dread each heart con - trol, what
soul, what ter - rors dread each heart con - trol, what
-way, Her that way bear, her that way bear, her
soul, what ter - rors dread each heart con - trol, what
soul, what ter - rors dread each heart con - trol, what
2d.

con - ster - na - tion fills each soul, ... a - way,..........
con - ster - na - tion fills each soul,........... a - way,........
that way bear, her that way bear,........... a - way,.. ....
con - ster - na - tion fills each soul,........... a - way,..........
con - ster - na - tion fills each soul,........... a - way,..........
.... a - way!..
.... a - way!..
.... a - way!..
.... a - way!..
.... a - way! ....

END OF ACT II.

ACT III.
INTRODUCTION.

A Magnificent Apartment, richly decorated with tapestry, mirrors, a portrait of the Virgin, &c.— (Doors R & L.) At the rear, a balcony, which overlooks the gardens of the distant palace.—Moonlight.—MARITANA discovered surveying the apartment.

"HOW DREARY TO MY HEART."

No. 22a. RECIT.

MARITANA.

How drea - ry to my heart, is this lone cham - ber! those crys - tal mir - rors, and those mar - ble halls, add to my gloom

While sweet - ly, sad re -

- membrance, the joy - ful hours of Lib - er - ty re - calls.

pp tremolo.

Poco piu lento.

My

lone - - ly form re - flect - ed as I pass, Seems

like a spec - tre, on my steps to wait. *Vivo.*

ad lib.

En - qu'r - ing from the gold en - wreathed glass,

Can mighty gran - deur be thus des - o - late!

Lento.

No. 22 b

Cantabile e con molta semplicità.

Scenes that are bright - - est, May charm...... a - - while, ... Hearts which are light - - est And eyes ..... that smile: Yet o'er them, a - bove us, Tho'...... na - ture beam,..... With none........ to love us, How sad............ they seem,........ With *ritard.*

none...... · to love us, How sad............ they seem!

Words can - not scat - - ter The

thoughts we fear,...... For tho' they flat - - ter, They mock ..... the

ear. Hopes will still de - - ceive us, With ..... tear - ful cost,...... And

dim.

Ped.

when........ *they* leave us, The heart......... is lost,........ And

[Exit R. H. D. *Noise of a carriage heard.]*

ritard.

when...... *they* leave us, The heart......... is lost.

pp

[Enter LAZARILLO. *From balcony.]*

LAZ. Madame, from the balcony, I perceive a carriage; it is Don Jose de—eh! not here! I see—again plunged in melancholy. What can this mystery be? and who is yonder lady, so secluded?—A prisoner in this palace.

[Enter DON JOSE. L. H. D.]

D. JOSE. Lazarillo!

LAZ. Signor. (*Bowing*)

D. JOSE. (*In an under tone.*) Where's the lady?

LAZ. (*Points off the stage.* R.) There, signor.

D. JOSE. Um! You saw the cavalier who spoke to me yesterday? Did you know his features?

LAZ. Yes, signor; they are stamped on every piastre in Spain—it was the King.

D. JOSE. True—but mind you make no mistake; nevertheless, if your memory fail in the least, look on this likeness, (*gives him gold.*) and when he comes here to-night—

LAZ. The King, signor?

D. JOSE. (*Whispers.*) Aye, boy, the King—mind, none else must be admitted.

LAZ. Should any other attempt?

D. JOSE. Desire him, from the lattice, there, to depart; if he refuse, be ready with your arquebuss, and fire at him.

LAZ. I obey, signor. (*Bows and exits, balcony.*)

D. JOSE. Having no real authority for the detention of Don Cæsar, he is, unfortunately, still at liberty, and in Madrid; luckily, however, his ignorance of the King's pardon will keep him out of the way, for fear of a re-apprehension; and the King, amused by the sparkling eyes of the Gitana, will utterly forget the beauteous Queen, that bright idol which he no longer worships, but for one of whose sweet smiles Don Jose would bow gladly perish.

"THIS HEART BY WOE O'ERTAKEN."

No. 23.

Lento e molto cantabile.

D. José.

This heart by woe o'er - tak - - en, Since love, since love rejects its pray - er, By

joy's last hope.... for - sa - - ken, Sinks in des - pair,.... lost in despair, In deep des-

rall.

- pair. This heart by woe o'ertaken, Since love rejects its

prayer, By joy's.... last hope, by hope for-sak-en, Sinks in des pair, sinks lost in deep des-

- pair.... This heart by woe o'er-tak--en, Since love, since love rejects its pray-er, By

joy's last hope.... for-sa--ken, Sinks in des-pair,.... lost in despair, in deep des-

rall.

- pair. This heart.................. by woe o'er -
8va
pp
- tak - - en, Since love re - jects, since love re - jects its
8va
rit.
rit.
pray'r...... By joy's last hope, last hope for - sa - ken, Sinks in des - pair, in deep des-
- pair, By joy's last hope for - sa - ken, Sinks, lost in deep des -
p

pair,........ Sinks in des - pair, in deep des - pair, Sinks, lost in deep des-pair.

Allegro ma non troppo.

No! my courage now re - gaining, Ban - ner waving, trumpet sounding, Nobly dar - ing, my gage maintain - ing, Forward, heart of Chi - val - ry, Forward, heart of Chi - val-

- ry. So the wounded knight un - tir - ing,

vibrato appassionato.

On his gal - lant steed re - bound - ing, At his la - dy's feet ex - pir - ing,

Dies for love and vic-to - ry. At his la - dy's feet ex - pir - ing, Dies for love and vic - to-

No! my courage now re - gaining, Ban - ner waving, trumpet sounding, Nobly dar - ing, my gage maintain - ing, Forward, heart of Chi - val - ry, Forward, heart of Chi - val

- ry. So the wounded knight un - tir - ing,

vibrato appassionato.

On his gal - lant steed re - bound - ing, At his la - dy's feet ex - pir - ing,

Dies for love and vic-to - ry. At his la - dy's feet ex - pir - ing, Dies for love and vic-to-

- ry, Dies for love and vic - to - ry, Dies for love and vic - to - ry..............

(Re-enter MARITANA, R.)

MARI. That voice!

D. JOSE. Ah! the Countess—

MARI. You! Oh, do not mock me by that title.

D. JOSE Nay, it is your own, but you appear uneasy; have I not kept my word? *(Smiling.)*

MARI. *(despondingly.)* Perfectly. I am a Countess,—I reside in a costly palace. Every desire of my proud heart, save one, has come to pass.

D. JOSE. And that one is, your husband? *(Making a signal off the stage, L.)* Your cup of delight is now brimful, your husband arrives.

(Enter LAZARILLO, showing in the KING, L.H.D.)

MARI. Husband! he? *(Retreats.)*

[D. JOSE *retires with* LAZARILLO

KING, *(detaining her.)* Lovely Maritana, do not fly me. Wherefore tremble? Fear'st thou me?

MARI. *(sighing.)* Indeed, yes!

KING. Thou art unhappy?

MARI. *(sadly.)* Indeed, indeed; yes!

KING. Wherefore?

MARI. Pardon! This strange marriage—thou, so exalted, I so humble!

KING, *(frowning.)* I exalted! Who hath told thee?

MARI. That brow severe—that lofty bearing; yes, yes, I feel so high thou art, I tremble to raise to thee one inquiring look.

KING. Courage, sweet Maritana! Were the earth at my command, I'd give thee all. Don Jose told me thou would'st fondly receive my affection.

MARI. Don Jose falsely rear'd this delusion, haply to enrich himself with thy wealth.

KING. Wealth! and thou would'st possess it also, shall flow like the golden shower of Danae into thy lap.

MARI. I—I disregard affluence.

KING. Nay, Maritana; doth it grieve thee thy husband is endowed with riches?

MARI. Willingly would I share poverty with one who shared my heart.

KING, *(tenderly.)* Listen to me, beautiful Maritana—listen!

MARI. You *are* my lord—I must obey.

KING. Obey! Oh, it is too cold a word. *(A shot heard.)* An intruder into the presence of—*(checking himself.)* Go in till this be past; I'll follow soon, believe.

MARI. *(aside.)* Ah me! unlucky Maritana. *(Exit, R.H.D.)*

KING, *(looking after her.)* The prize is mine! at length she believes all—all. *(DON CÆSAR appears in balcony.)*

KING. Ah! a man here! *(Stands aside to observe.)*

(LAZARILLO fires again without.)

D. CÆSAR. That's one way of receiving a gentleman, by sending a bullet through his brains!

(Enter LAZARILLO, BALCONY, the arquebuss in his hand.)

D. CÆSAR, *(looking about.)* Eh? who knows me? *(Sees the KING.)* Pardon, Signor, I did not perceive you.

KING. Why come you in at the window?

D. CÆSAR. Refused admittance at the door, the window was the only way. Egad! a man needs a stout courage to storm a fortress under such a brisk cannonade. *(Shaking a bullet from his hat.)* It is but to show the tip of one's feather above yon corridor, and whiz comes a bullet at your head. Spirit of Hospitality, how are thy rights abused!

KING, *(sternly.)* I am master here, and insist on knowing your motive for this intrusion.

D. CÆSAR. Well, then, since you are master of the house, I come to seek the Countess de Bazan! They say she lives here!

KING. The Countess? Do you know her?

D. CÆSAR. Ha! ha! ha! She's the acquaintance of ten minutes only;—but if you *are* master here, tell me where to find her?

KING, *(indignantly.)* I tell! I! Are you aware signor, that I am—

D. CÆSAR. Who?

KING, *(in confusion.)* Wh—o! Don Cæsar de Bazan! *(Seating himself.)*

D. CÆSAR, *(aside.)* Parbleu! I must chastise this impostor. *(Touches his sword.)*

LAZ. *(appearing at the balcony.)* It is the King! *(Aside and disappears.)*

D. CÆSAR. Ha! The King! here, at this hour!

KING. And who, signor, pray may you happen to be? Your name!—

D. CÆSAR. My name! Oh, if *you* are Don Cæsar de Bazan, *(putting on his hat,)* I am the King of Spain!

KING, *(rising.)* You! King of—ha! ha! ha!

I AM THE KING OF SPAIN.

No. 24. DUET. Don Cæsar and King.

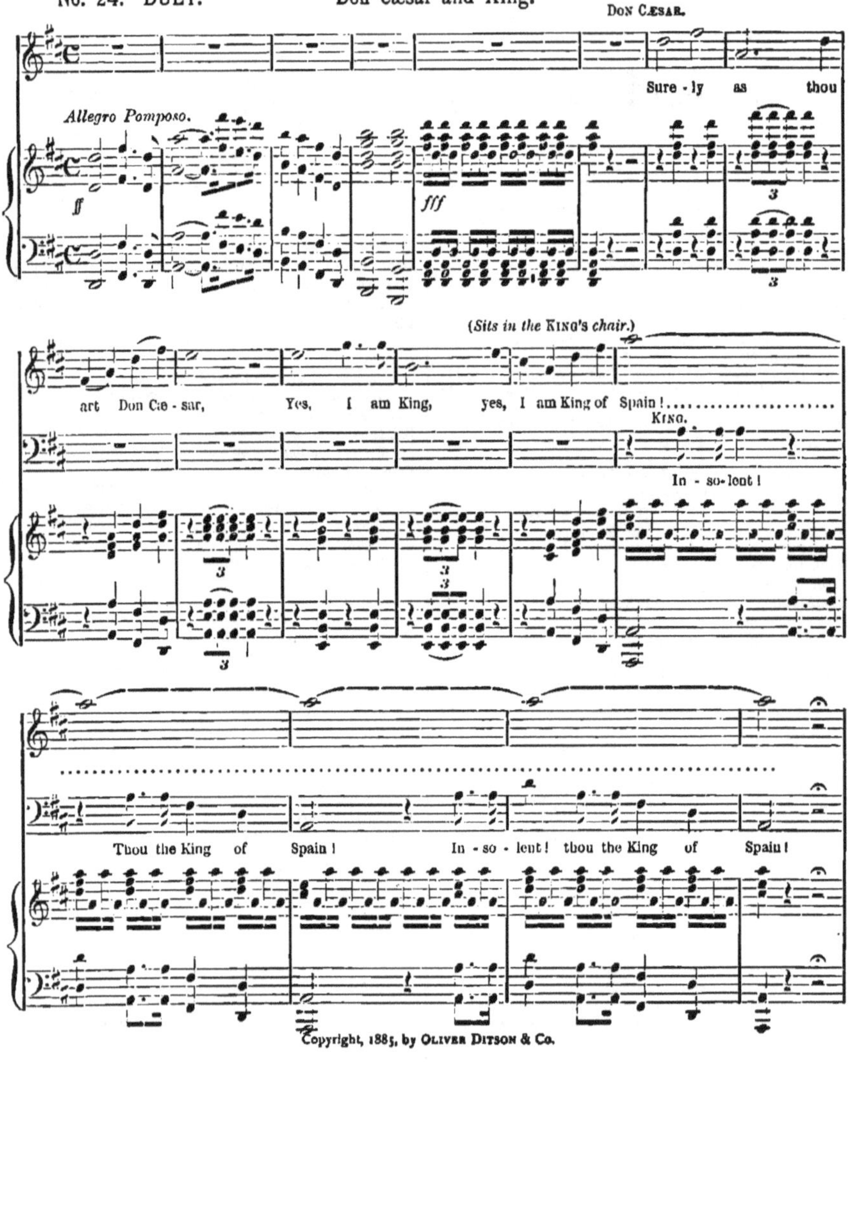

KING. *(Aside.)*

I can't my mirth re - strain, I can't my

ritard.   *Allegretto Scherzoso.*

mirth restrain. I can't my mirth re - - strain.

DON CÆSAR. (*With sarcasm.*)

You mar - vel, Signor,   at   this hour   we un - at - tended ... here are seen,..... 80

near a pret - ty woman's door, that woman too, is not   the   Queen!   But Kings, you know, like

other men, some-times   a lit - tle   thus give way; Kings are   but mor - tal, Don Cæ - sar,   Of

(Reflecting.)

course, you'll not your King be - tray,......... ... ...Don Cæ - sar now I re - mem - ber well, a wit - ty,

of course! of course!

brawling, mad - brain'd sot I.... Be - neath his weap - on 'twas that fell the Cap - tain of our guard, was't

not ?.... Be kind enough to make it clear, If shot as or - der'd t'oth - er day, and be - ing dead, How came you here? Of course, I shall not you be - tray. ....

KING.

Of course! of course! But

piu mosso.

What, for- get, we?

Sire,.... your mem - o - ry is short, ... a most im - por - tant, a most im - por - tant

piu mosso.

thing,.... Don Cæ - sar ... at eight o'clock re - ceiv'd, ... receiv'd the

pp *cres.*

ad lib.
Don Cæsar. (Aside, smiling.)
par - don, the par - don of the King.............. Un - hap - py fate!............ un - hap - py
ad lib.
fate!.................... The par - don ar - riv'd....... at eight, ... un - hap - py
rall.
fate!.................. un - hap - py fate!................ and I was shot, ... was
King.
shot. .. at sev - - en. You to de - nounce .... me were...... too

late,............ you to de - nounce me were.... too late,.................... you

see............. I am for-giv - - en!.... you see... I am........ for-

-giv - en! you to de - nounce.......... me were too late,.............. you see I

Tempo 1mo.

am, I am for-giv-en.

8va.....................

Tempo 1mo.

Don Cæsar.
King.
'Twere use - less lon - ger to re - tain a ti - tle not my own..... Then
8va
Sir,........ you are not King........ of Spain,........ Then
Sir,........ you are not King of Spain, you are not
8va
cres.
Don Cæsar.
piu vivo.
King of Spain, you are not King of Spain. No, I my
8va
piu vivo.

dig - ni - ty for - go, no, no, I own my ti - - tle vain, and doff my borrow'd plumes a -
KING. (*Bowing in mockery.*)

Ha! ha! I can't my mirth re -

8va

- gain, and doff my bor - row'd plumes a - gain, To cry... a - loud, vive King of Spain!

- strain, so ve - ry brief has been your reign, most High........ and migh - ty King of Spain!

8va *tr*

Allegro. *ff*

ff

f

Allegro.

.... vive King of Spain! To cry........ a - loud vive King of Spain! vive King of Spain! To

.... King of Spain, most high .... and migh - ty King of Spain, King of Spain, most cry a - - - loud........ vivo King........ ... of Spain! To

high and migh - - ty King............ of Spain! Most

cry a - - - loud............ .... vivo King............

high and migh - - - - - - ty King............

.... of Spain!.....

.... of Spain!.....

[*Enter* LAZARILLO. *From balcony*]

LAZ. Sire, in haste—a messenger. (*Gives King a paper.*)

KING. (*Reading it.*) Ah! from the Queen! Arrived there, at the Palace, and expecting me! just now, provoking! Boy, call thy fellows up, and order straight they thrust forth yon stranger, and if our heavy anger thou'dst not incur, see it instant done. [*Exit* L.

LAZ. Sire, I will! (*With remorse.*) My benefactor, Don Cæsar.

I had nearly shot you just now!

D. CÆSAR. Never mind, boy—where's the lady? (*Looking about.*)

LAZ. If you mean the mysterious lady who—Ah! here she comes! Oh, signor, beware! (*Alarmed.*)

D. CÆSAR. I must speak with her: watch; let no one interrupt us!

LAZ. Alas! what peril! [*Exit* L. H. L.

[*Enter* MARITANA R. H. D.]

"OH MARITANA."

No. 25. DUET.

Lyrics under the staves:

A stranger here! Is it thus, is it thus we meet?

That voice, that voice! Once more we meet! 'Tis the Zin - ga - ra! Yes, Ma - ri - ta - na.

Don Cæsar. *(with grief.)*

Oh, Mar - i - ta - na! wild wood - flow'r Did they but give thee a proud - er name,.... To place thee in a kingly bow- er, And deck thee, and

deck thee.... with a gild - ed shame! No, Ma - ri - ta - na,

though in this bow'r Lips the most pure shall nev - er blame!.... A

cap - tive in a stranger's pow-er Shall perish ere she yield, ere she yield to shame.

But who art thou, my

con - duct thus to scan? But who art thou, my

con - duct thus to scan?

Don Cæsar.
I am........ thy Hus - band, Don Cæsar de Ba - zan.
Maritana.
My
Maritana. (joyfully.)
rall.
Hus-band! yes! he is the man, yes,.... my Hus - band,
Don Cæsar.
Thy Hus-band! yes! I am the man........ yes,.... thy Hus - band,
pp
rall.
dim.
never-more to part, Thine ... for - ev - er, is this faith - ful heart, Ah!
pp
never-more to part, Thine.... for - ev - er, is this faith - ful heart,
piu vivo.

thine for - ev - er is this faith-ful heart.

Ah! live for - ev - er

Ah!...... yes........ my Hus - band, nev- er-more to

in this faith - ful heart .... yes........ thy Hus-band, nev- er-more to

part........ yes, thine........ for - ev - er is this faithful heart,

part........ yes, thine........ for - ev - er is this faithful heart,

rall.

colla voce.

pp

Thine for - ev - er is this faith - ful heart. Thine for - ev - er

Live for - ev - er In this faith - ful heart, Live for - ev - er

is........... this faith - - - ful heart.......................

in........... this faith - - - ful heart....... ....

colla voce.

morendo.

Recit. MARITANA.

But first to prove it? Dost thou re-member those words which at the altar thou said'st to me.

ad lib.

p

moderato.

DON CÆSAR.

Yes, yes, I'll prove it, I said, "Re-member, The rest of my ex - is - tence I de-vote to thee! The rest of my ex - is - tence I de-vote to thee!

rall.

lento. pp

Allegro. MARITANA.

thee! Yes, yes, oh joy! 'Tis he! 'tis

Don Caesar.
he! Thy hus - band!
Maritana.
My Husband! Thine..
Don Caesar.
Yes, Thine........... ....
Allegro moderato.
This heart with joy............ o'er - flow - ing, Like
This joy my heart.......... o'er - flow - ing, Like

nec - tar - sparkling wine............ In sun - lit crys - tal glow - ing Seems in -
nec - tar - sparkling wine............ Sweet mag - ic round me throw - ing, Wakes in
- spir'd by rays di - vine. This heart with joy o'er-
ec - sta - cy di - vine. This joy my heart o'er
- flow - ing. In - spired by rays di - vine, yes, This
- flow - ing. Like nec - tar-spark - ling wine, yes, This
3
f
f

heart with joy.... ..o'er-flow - ing Like nec - tar like nec-tar-spark - ling wine, In

joy my heart o'er-flow - ing Like nec - tar, like nec-tar-spark - ling wine, Sweet

sun - lit crys - tal glow - ing seems in - spired by rays........ di - vine, by rays di -

mag - ic round me throw - ing wakes in ec - sta - cy........ di - vine, in ec - sta -

- vine, by rays di - vine, by rays di - vine ..... (They embrace.)

- cy, in ec - sta - cy, in ec - sta - cy di - vine...............

(Enter LAZARILLO. L. H. D.)

LAZ. Fly, signor, guards approach the palace!

MARI. *(troubled.)* Save thyself! Escape!

D. CÆSAR. Leave thee, my wife! the King at thy chamber door!

MARI. In yonder garden walketh the Queen, I saw her from the lattice above! Fly to her feet, tell her that poor Mari-tana is here, a captive, in peril—she will rescue me!

D. CÆSAR, She—this sword—

MARI. No, no; the Queen *alone* can, will save me! if you love me, do as I entreat!—to the Queen! to the Queen!

D. CÆSAR. To the Queen!

Exit by the window—she turns to the portrait of the Virgin, and falls on her knees.)

SAINTED MOTHER.

No. 26. DUET.

Maritana and Lazarillo.

Lento.

MARITANA.

Saint - - - ed Moth - - er, guide .... his foot - - steps,

Guide them at a mo - ment, guide them at a mo - - ment sure ....

LAZARILLO.

Saint - - - ed Moth - - er, guide .... his foot - - steps,

MARITANA.

LAZARILLO.

Let the guide them at a mo--ment, at a mo-ment, a mo-ment sure, Let the

wick--ed heart then per-ish, And the good,.... the good remain se-cure. Saint-ed

wick--ed heart then per-ish, And the good,.... the good remain se-cure. Sainted

Moth--er, oh! be-friend him, And thy gent-lest pi-ty lend him!

Moth--er, oh! be-friend him, And thy gent-lest pi-ty lend him!

LAZARILLO.

Ah! Saint - ed Moth - - er, guide .... his ... foot - steps, Ah!

guide them at a mo - - ment, at a mo - - ment sure.

MARITANA.

Ah! Saint - ed Moth - - er, guide .... his foot - steps, Ah!

MARITANA.

guide them at a mo - - ment, guide them at a mo - - ment sure. Let the wick - ed heart then per - ish. Let the wick - ed heart.. then per - ish. Sainted

Let the wick - ed,........ Let the wick - ed heart then per - ish. Sainted

Moth - er, oh !..... be - friend him, ... And thy gentlest, and.... thy gentlest pit - y

Moth - er, oh ! be - friend him, ... And thy gentlest, and.... thy gentlest pit - y

lend him. Let the wick - ed heart then per - ish, Let the wick - ed heart then

lend him. Let the wick - ed,........ Let the wick - ed heart then per - ish, Saint - ed Moth - - er, oh! ..... be - friend him, ... And thy

per - ish, Saint - ed Moth - - er, oh! ..... be - friend him, ... And thy

a piacere.

gentlest, and thy gent - lest pit - - y lend him, And thy gent - lest, thy gent - lest

gentlest, and.... thy gent - lest pit - - y lend him, And thy gent - lest, thy gent - lest

pit - - - y lend .... him.

pit - - - y lend .... him.

LAZARILLO That stop! It is the King! (*Retires, BALCONY.*)
(*Enter the KING.—Re-enter DON CÆSAR, L.H.D., who locks the door.*)
KING. Why lock'st thou the door?
D. CÆSAR. That none else bear, what now I dare to utter; thou art my King—thou'st my dishonor sought—my wife insulted—thus I, that wrong repay! (*Throwing down his sword.*)
KING. Intruder! What ho!—who waiteth?
LARITANA. To death they'll drag thee!—by the lattice fly!
{ D. CÆSAR, (*to KING.*) Sire, an instant bear me! *
{ KING, (*with emotion.*) Away! I spare thy life.
D. CÆSAR. Sire, I bear a mission.
KING. A mission!—thou? From whom?
D. CÆSAR. Sire, from the Queen! who would save Maritana!
KING. How! did they dare admit thee to the presence of her Majesty?

D. CÆSAR. No, Sire, they did *not* admit me by the portal, therefore climbed I the garden wall, resolved to cast myself, unlooked for, at her Majesty's feet.
KING, (*angrily.*) What sought you of the Queen? Audacious!
D. CÆSAR. To save my wife: that effort saved my King!
KING. Thy King!
D. CÆSAR. At least, his honor! To avoid the notice of the guards, hidden behind the foliage, I heard, in converse deep, two voices, a woman's and a man's. Shall I go on?
KING. Proceed.
D. CÆSAR. "Madam, you are betrayed," said the cavalier to the lady; "the King to-night meeteth his mistress in yonder villa."
KING. And that traitor was—
D. CÆSAR. Don Jose!
KING. And the lady?
D. CÆSAR. The Queen.
KING. The Queen! Oh, shame!

"REMORSE AND DISHONOR."

No. 27. TRIO.
Andante.

* No. 19, originally introduced here, when not sung, omit the lines enclosed in brackets.

heart. Re - morse and dis - hon - or Their an - guish im - part, Oh! may they sub-

D. CÆSAR. (L.)

If shame and dis - hon - or Such tor - tures im - part, Oh! what can re-

KING. (R.)

Oh! shame and dis - hon - or Such an - guish im - part, Oh! what can re-

- due him, and van - quish his heart.

- quite us for guilt in the heart.

- quite us for guilt in the heart. Shame and dis - hon - or such an - guish im-

Re - morse and dis - hon - or their an-guish im - part, Oh! may they sub-

If shame and dis-

- part. Oh! shame and dis-

- due him, Oh! may they sub - due him, Oh! may they sub - due .... him and

- hon - or, If shame and dis - hon - or, If shame and dis - hon - - or such

- hon - or, If shame and dis - hon - or, If shame and dis - hon - - or such

van - - quish.... his heart. Oh! may they sub - due him and van - quish his
tor - - tures.... im - part. Oh! what can re - quite us, for guilt in the
an - - guish im - part. It seems as a ser - pent were twin'd round my
heart, Oh! may they sub - due him and van - quish his heart, Ah........
heart! Oh! what can re - quite us, for guilt in the heart, for
heart, It seems as a ser - pent were twin'd round my heart, were

tr
pp
Ah.............................. Remorse and dis - hon - or, Their
guilt, for guilt, in the heart.............................. If shame and dis - hon - or, Such
twin'd, were twin'd round my heart.............................. Oh! shame and dis - hon - or, Such
an - guish im - part; Oh! may they sub - due him and van - quish his
tor - tures im - part; Ah! what can re - quite us, for guilt in the
an - guish im - part; It seems as a ser - pent were twin'd round my

heart.

Poco piu mosso.

heart!   If   shame   and   dis - hon - or   Such tor - tures im-

heart.

- part....   Ah! what   can re - quite us,   for guilt in   the

Ah! what can re - quite us, Ah! what can re -
heart?
Ah! what can re - quite us, Ah! what can re -

pp
- quite us, What can re - quite us, for guilt in the
pp
What can re - quite us, for guilt in the
pp
- quite us, What can re - quite us, for guilt in the
pp

heart! Ah! what can re- - quite us, For

heart! Ah! what can re - quite us, For

heart! Ah! what can re - quite us, For

stringendo.

guilt in the heart! For guilt in the heart!

guilt in the heart! For guilt in the heart!

guilt in the heart! For guilt in the heart!

pp
what can re - quite, Ah! what can re - quite
pp
what can re - quite, Ah! what can re - quite
pp
what can re - quite, Ah! what can re - quite
pp
us, for guilt in the heart in the
us, for guilt in the heart in the
us, for guilt in the heart in the

pp ... **ff** ... **pp**

heart, for guilt in the heart, for guilt in the heart? for

heart, for guilt in the heart, for guilt in the heart? for

guilt in the heart, for guilt in the heart ....

guilt in the heart, for guilt, in the heart ....

KING, (*Crosses to* L.H.D.) Unlock the door, I say, and let me forth !

D CÆSAR. Sire, thou would'st arrive too late.

KING. Too late, say'st—

D. CÆSAR. Think'st thou Don Cæsar de Bazan spared the man, who, though scorned by his Queen, to whom he spoke of love, would have betrayed his King ? No, Sire ; by this true hand the traitor fell. I have done my utmost to preserve thine honor, can'st thou destroy mine ? (*Kneels.*)

KING, (*much affected, and making a sign to* MARITANA, *who gives him* DON CÆSAR's *sword.*) No, Don Cæsar, and may that loyal sword which has so preserved the dignity of your King, ever defend, with equal bravery, thine own. Rise ! I hear footsteps. *Now*, unlock the door. (DON

CÆSAU *unlocks the door.*)

(*Enter* LAZARILLO, OFFICERS, &c., *of the King's Household,* L H.D.)

NOBLE. Sire, we have sought you at the request of her Majesty.—

KING. And found us in the villa of the Count de Bazan one of our most loyal subjects. Don Cæsar de Bazan, we appoint you Governor of Grenada.

D. CÆSAR. Valentia is also vacant, Sire.

KING. Would *you* prefer Valentia to Grenada?

D. CÆSAR. Valentia is one hundred leagues from Madrid, Sire, and beyond the reach of my creditors.

KING, (*laughing.*) Well, well, Governor of Valentia, be it then !

WITH RAPTURE GLOWING.

No. 28. FINALE. King, (R.) Maritana, Don Cæsar, (C.) Lazarillo. (L.)

With rap - ture glowing, Bounds this heart o'er -
- flow- ing! With rap - ture glowing, Kind friends a - - round ap - prove......

With rap - ture glow - ing, Bounds this heart o'er - flow - ing!

With rap - ture glow - ing, Kind friends............ .... ap - prove: Hence with

sad - ness, welcome glad - ness, Love and treas - ure, wel - - come pleas - - ure,

Wel - come joy and peace,.............. welcome joy......................... and
love.
CHORUS.
Vi - va Ma - ri - - ta - - na, may thy name be great in sto - ry, may thy
Vi - va Ma - ri - - ta - - na, may thy name be great in sto - ry, may thy

Lyrics under the music:

fame be bright in glo - - ry, Ma-ri-ta - - - na, Vi - - va! Vi-

fame be bright in glo - - ry, Ma-ri-ta - - - na, Vi - - va! Vi-

-va! Vi - - - va! Vi-va, Vi-va, Vi-va, Vi-va.

-va! Vi - - - va! Vi-va, Vi-va, Vi-va, Vi-va.

With rap - ture glow - ing, Bounds this heart o'er -

- flow- ing! With rap - ture glowing, Kind friends a - - round ap - prove.....................

With rap - ture glow - ing, Bounds this heart o'er - flow - ing!

With rap - ture glow - ing, Kind friends............ ...... ap - prove: Hence with

sad - ness, welcome glad - ness, Love and treas - ure, wel - - come pleas - - ure,

wel - come joy and peace,....... welcome joy................................... and

love.
Vi - va Ma - ri - - ta - - - na, may thy name be great in sto - ry, may thy
Vi - va Ma - ri - - ta - - - na, may thy name be great in sto - ry, may thy
f
O joy O
fame be bright in glo - - ry, Ma-ri - ta - - - na, Vi - - va, Vi - va, Vi -
fame be bright in glo - - - ry, Ma-ri - ta - - - na, Vi - - va, Vi - va, Vi -
ff

joy... and love!...........

.va, Vi - va, Vi - va, Vi - va, Vi - va, Vi - va, Vi - va...........

.va, Vi - va, Vi - va, Vi - va, Vi - va, Vi - va, Vi - va...........

_ff_